Shaykh Mufid

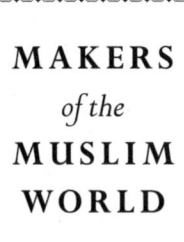

MAKERS
of the
MUSLIM
WORLD

Shaykh Mufid

TAMIMA BAYHOM-DAOU

ONEWORLD
OXFORD

SHAYKH MUFID

Oneworld Publications
(Sales and editorial)
185 Banbury Road
Oxford OX2 7AR
England
www.oneworld-publications.com

ISBN 1–85168–383–6

Typeset by Jayvee, India
Cover and text design by Design Deluxe
Printed and bound in India by Thomson Press Ltd
on acid-free paper

CONTENTS

Preface vii

1 **INTRODUCTION** 1
   The Sunni–Shi'i Divide 1
   Imami Shi'ism: an Outline of Main Developments 4

2 **THE TIMES AND CAREER OF MUFID** 17
   The Buyids 18
   Imamism under the Buyids 19
   Other Religious Groups 21
   The Career of Mufid 27

3 **THE IMAMATE: THE HISTORICAL ARGUMENTS** 31
   The Mainstream Historical Tradition 33
   The Imamate of 'Ali 35
   The Other Imams 46

4 **THE IMAMATE: THE RATIONAL ARGUMENTS** 55
   The Necessity of the Imamate 56
   The Imams' Infallibility 58
   The Imams' Knowledge 60
   The Imams and the Qur'an 63
   The Imams' Miracles 67
   The Imams after Death 68

Unacceptable Exaggeration 70
The Occultation of the Twelfth Imam 75

5 THEOLOGY 83

Mu'tazili Theology 84
Sunni Theology 89
Early Imamism between Reason and Revelation 91
Mufid and the Role of Reason 95
The Dogmas of Imamism 98

6 JURISPRUDENCE 111

The Principles of Imami Jurisprudence 112
The Jurist as Deputy of the Imam 121
Ritual Practices and Laws Specific to Imamism:
    Emblems of Communal Identity 130

7 CONCLUSION 135

Further Reading 139
Index 141

PREFACE

The purpose of this book is to introduce the thought of an Imami Shi'i scholar who lived and worked in Baghdad at the turn of the eleventh century and was the first of a line of scholars who helped establish a role for human reasoning in the elaboration of Imami doctrine.

Muhammad ibn Muhammad ibn al-Nu'man al-Harithi al-'Ukbari al-Baghdadi, more commonly known as al-Shaykh al-Mufid (the "instructive or teaching scholar," a title referring to his great learning), was the leading Imami scholar of his day. He was a prolific author, teacher, and dedicated defender of Imami beliefs. He flourished at a time when Shi'ism, the religion of a persecuted minority for most of its early history, was enjoying political support in many areas of the Muslim world, but also when Imamism, the Shi'i sect he belonged to, was facing major intellectual challenges, both from within and from rival religious groups, and needed to be defined and defended along new theoretical lines. Mufid laid down the theoretical foundations of an Imami legal system and a theology capable of competing with other systems and schools of Islamic thought. He wrote extensively in defense of the Imami view of early Islamic history and of the particular dogmas and laws of his sect.

Imami Shi'ism in the time of Mufid was consolidating itself as a semi-autonomous religious community within Islam, and its scholars or jurists were becoming increasingly involved in the management of its social affairs. The scholars were also beginning to legitimize their role on the basis that some of the functions of their supreme leader, the occulted imam of the time, had been delegated to them. (The belief that the imam of the time, the only legitimate ruler and source of religious authority, was in a state of occultation had been a main distinguishing feature of Imamism since the late ninth century.) Mufid contributed to the process of legitimizing the social role of the scholars, a process which in our own time ended with Khomeini's doctrine that in the absence of the imam the ideal ruler was the leading jurist.

Mufid is still highly esteemed among Imamis. In 1413/1992 Imami communities celebrated his millenary and an international conference was held in the Iranian town of Qumm. His extant works have been collected and published in a series with the approval of the select committee supervising the conference, making them more accessible.

In order to understand Mufid's contribution and the role he played as the leading scholar of his community, it is necessary to give a description of the main developments and trends in early Imamism, and especially in the period leading up to his own time. In presenting an outline of those developments I have followed a line of interpretation based partly on long-established research and partly on more recent findings, including my own. It must be pointed out here that some aspects of early Imami history are still matters of debate among scholars. This book is not the place to engage in those debates. Only where an issue is directly relevant to the assessment of Mufid's contribution has there been some discussion of it here.

In citing the Qur'an, I have used the form "Q. chapter number: verse number." The verse numbering follows that of the official Egyptian edition. The dates and centuries given are according to the Muslim Hijri and the Christian CE calendars and in the form "Hijri/CE."

I should like to thank Robert Gleave, Patricia Crone, and Oneworld's anonymous reader for their help and useful comments on an earlier draft of this book. Needless to say, none of them is in any way responsible for its mistakes and shortcomings.

INTRODUCTION

THE SUNNI–SHI'I DIVIDE

Shaykh Mufid was a Shi'i of the Imamiyya, which is also known as the Ithna'ashariyya or Twelver Shi'ism. Like the other two main branches of Shi'ism, the Zaydiyya and the Isma'iliyya, the Imamiyya had come to be distinguished from mainstream Sunni Islam by its views on the question of authority within the Muslim community.

There were two aspects to this question. The first may be defined as political and concerned the question of leadership of the community and succession to the Prophet, that is to say, the caliphate or, as it was referred to in religious discussions, the imamate. The Sunnis argued that the Prophet had made no provisions for his succession and it was left up to the community to choose and agree upon a successor. They regarded the first four caliphs, including 'Ali, the Prophet's cousin and son-in-law, as rightly guided (*rashidun*) imams whose acts and decisions were binding precedents. They accepted all subsequent caliphs as legitimate, though not necessarily also righteous, rulers. In their view, those caliphs derived their legitimacy from being descended from the Prophet's tribe of Quraysh and from the fact that they were able to hold the community together and allow Islam to flourish; they (or most of them) did not, however, fulfil the conditions of the rightly guided caliphate, and it was not expected that the ideal caliphate could one day be restored.

By contrast, most of the Shi'a believed that 'Ali, who ruled as fourth caliph, had been the only legitimate ruler, and that the caliphate ought to have passed to his descendants from Fatima, the Prophet's daughter. All the other caliphs were regarded as usurpers. The rights of the 'Alids were said to have been based mainly on the Prophet's designation of 'Ali as his successor. According to the Imami Shi'a, those rights were transmitted in a hereditary line of twelve successive imams, eleven of whom had each designated (nass) a successor. The twelfth and last of the line, a figure whose very existence was questioned by opponents as he was never seen by outsiders, was believed to have gone into a state of occultation (ghayba) in the year 260/874. His return to rule the world as the Mahdi, the Islamic redeemer, will be at the end of time. The fact that of the twelve imams only 'Ali had actually become caliph, and that most of his successors did not actively claim the caliphate, did not invalidate their right to it.

In Isma'ili Shi'ism the line of recognized imams branched off from the Imami line after the sixth imam, Ja'far al-Sadiq, and continued from his son Isma'il down to the Fatimid caliphs (and eventually to their successors). As in Imamism, the Isma'ili line was constituted by the designation of each imam by his predecessor. In Zaydi Shi'ism, on the other hand, any of the descendants of 'Ali and Fatima who laid claim to the imamate and rebelled against the ruling authorities was recognized as rightful imam (provided he had the requisite religious learning).

The other issue over which Sunni and Shi'i Islam were divided was that of religious authority, the authority to define and interpret the revealed law of Islam or the shari'a which regulates all aspects of Muslim life. According to both, religious authority was based mainly on knowledge of the Prophet

Muhammad's legacy, the Qur'an and the Sunna, that is, the Prophet's law or practice as preserved in Hadith reports about his words and deeds. But whereas the Sunnis maintained that after the death of the Prophet that authority was dispersed among his companions and followers and eventually came to be held by the religious scholars, most Shi'is asserted that it passed on to 'Ali and the imams after him.

In Imami and Isma'ili Shi'ism the imams were believed to be the most knowledgeable of all Muslims, by virtue of their infallibility ('isma), access to divine inspiration (ilham), and knowledge ('ilm) transmitted exclusively to them from the Prophet. The necessity of having an imam at all times to act as guide to mankind was a fundamental belief in both. In Isma'ilism this belief had a practical aspect in that the line of imams was visible and continuing (in fact, it continues to the present day in the person of the Agha Khan). In Imamism, on the other hand, the necessary existence of the imam was (or, by the early fourth/tenth century, had come to be) a purely theological concept: the twelfth imam, who existed in a state of occultation, was the ultimate and perpetual source of religious authority in this world, but the Imami scholars were the effective holders of that authority, much the same as their Sunni counterparts. The difference was that whereas the Sunni scholars relied on the transmitted statements and views of the Prophet and his revered companions, the Imami scholars relied on the transmitted teachings of their imams, which for them represented the only true version of the Sunna of the Prophet and contained the only true interpretation of the Qur'an.

The Zaydi imam was also looked upon as a religious guide and the most learned member of the community but, unlike the Imami and Isma'ili imams, he was not credited with infallibility or access to divine sources of knowledge. His knowledge was based mainly on Hadith transmitted by other descendants of the Prophet, all of whom were believed by Zaydis to have a special ability to acquire and preserve his heritage.

IMAMI SHI'ISM: AN OUTLINE OF MAIN DEVELOPMENTS

The three Shi'i traditions described here trace the origins of their doctrines to the time of the Prophet and the early caliphate. Modern research suggests, however, that they did not begin to crystallize as sects with clearly defined ideas about the nature and role of the imamate until much later: the latter part of the second/eighth century in the case of Imami and Zaydi Shi'ism, and a hundred or so years later in the case of Isma'ilism. But the roots of Shi'ism may be located in earlier periods.

Devotion to the Prophet's Family

Support for 'Ali originated in Kufa, a garrison town in southern Iraq, during the reign of his predecessor, the unpopular third caliph, 'Uthman. It continued during 'Ali's reign as caliph, when he was engaged in conflicts with other members of the ruling elite. During the time of the Umayyad caliphs, when the empire was ruled from Damascus (between 41/661 and 132/749), this support developed into a movement of opposition centered in Iraq. It was characterized by allegiance to the Family of the Prophet (that is, his kinsmen) and the belief that they alone had a legitimate claim to the caliphate. Originally, the Family of the Prophet referred to the whole clan of Hashim (the Prophet's ancestor), but succession was gradually narrowed down to the 'Alids, and then to the descendants of the Prophet through 'Ali and Fatima.

Shi'i Messianism

Shi'ism in the Umayyad period was not only about support for the Prophet's kinsmen as rightful caliphs. Messianic expectations and beliefs, centered on one or the other member of the Family, became rife within it. These did not always differ from the messianic beliefs found among mainstream Muslims. The latter, like the Shi'is, tended to use the name Mahdi (the Rightly Guided One) for the Islamic redeemer and also conceived of him mainly as a political figure who was expected to "fill the earth with justice."

But Shi'i messianism came to be distinguished by two closely related ideas: the "absence" (or occultation) of the Mahdi; and his "return" from death or from a supernatural occultation on earth or in heaven. The circumstances of his return were described in apocalyptic terms. He was often referred to as the Qa'im, a term said to refer to his "rising" from the dead or with the sword. (In Samaritanism the same term denoted the "Standing One," a priestly messiah who never dies.)

A Quietist and Legalist Current

In addition to the messianic currents, there was beginning to emerge within Shi'ism a quietist and scholarly trend centered around certain members of the 'Alid family, who were known to have shunned involvement in politics and occupied themselves with religious learning. The most prominent among them were Muhammad al-Baqir (d. 117/735) and Ja'far al-Sadiq (d. 148/765), who are recognized as the fifth and the sixth Imami imams. These two figures were widely recognized even beyond Shi'i circles for their learning and piety. They had a number of Sunni and Shi'i disciples and pupils who sought their opinion on legal and dogmatic matters. Their importance in Imamism is attested by the fact that the bulk of Imami Hadith is traced back to them. Yet it is unlikely that they were regarded as Imami imams, in the sense of sole authority on religious matters, in their own lifetime.

The idea of the imamate as a permanent religious office based on designation and not dependent on actual possession of political power is well attested for the first time in the latter part of the second/eighth century, during the time of Ja'far's son Musa al-Kazim (d. 183/799). Its emergence may be related to the need felt in some pro-'Alid scholarly circles to shed the messianic legacy of Shi'ism and redefine it along new lines. After the advent of the 'Abbasid dynasty there were a number of messianically inspired revolts against it by 'Alids or their supporters, all of which ended in failure. Many 'Alid Shi'is would have soon realized that insurrection and bloodshed were not going to lead anywhere and that a change of dynasty was not likely to bring about any significant change in government. For some scholars a depoliticized Shi'ism would have been one way of accommodating themselves to the reality of 'Abbasid rule and, at the same time, maintaining their devotion to the 'Alids. Ja'far's and his father Muhammad's quietism and their interest in scholarship would have helped to promote the idea that this line of 'Alids was endowed with a special ability to transmit the heritage of the Prophet. Moreover, in some scholarly circles the existence within Islam of divergent opinions on numerous questions of law and dogma was perceived as something of a problem. The Imami imamate was presented to Muslims as the answer to divergence.

By the third/ninth century Imamism had spread from Iraq to several towns of eastern Iran (Nishapur, Tus, Samarqand) and western Iran (Rayy, Qumm, Nihawand, Hamadan, and Qazwin). It remained though the religion of a small minority until the tenth/sixteenth century when the Safavid dynasty of Iran made it the state religion.

The quietism advocated in Imamism may in the long run have helped its communities to survive in main centers of the Islamic empire and in the midst of predominantly Sunni populations. But it did not protect Imamis from attack or prevent their imams from being suspected of plotting to seize power and kept under house arrest. The usual pretext for their Sunni attackers was that Imamism vilified the first three caliphs and other companions of the Prophet who did not recognize 'Ali's claims, that is to say, those whom the Sunnis regarded as the pious founders of the community. To protect themselves against such hostility, Imamis found refuge in the idea of precautionary dissimulation (taqiyya), that a Muslim is allowed to conceal his faith if by revealing it he would be subjecting himself to danger or persecution. In time this idea became a fundamental element of Imami belief.

Early Imami Doctrine of the Imamate

By comparison with classical Imamism (viz., Imamism as the set of beliefs that had emerged by the end of the third/ninth century and that remained the basis of all later formulations), early Imami doctrine of the imamate was a very moderate one. It was based on two related ideas: that the revelation to the Prophet Muhammad, then conceived strictly as the Qur'an and its interpretation, was a complete and perfect source of the religious law; and that the continued existence of a single line of infallible and divinely guided imams guaranteed the perfect transmission of that knowledge. It was said that each imam received that knowledge through transmission from his predecessor (and, in the case of 'Ali, from the Prophet), and divine guidance insured that he did not err in its transmission. At first, the imam was not thought to be in receipt of additional divinely imparted knowledge (ilham). On the contrary, early Imamis adhered strictly to the view that all divine communication came to an end with the death of the Prophet.

The Threat of Extremism

By the early part of the third/ninth century Imamism was already beginning to face a threat to its existence as a moderate expression of Shi'ism from individuals and groups preaching gnostic or quasi-gnostic doctrines. Gnostic currents had flourished in Iraq and Iran in late antiquity and were now resurfacing mainly in Shi'ism. The central idea in gnosticism was that the salvation of the human soul was from the material world and lay in the acquisition of esoteric or secret knowledge about its divine origins and destiny. This could be achieved by recognizing a savior who was usually conceived of as an incarnation of a celestial being or of the divine essence, and whose role was essentially that of awakener and revealer of gnosis.

Imami scholars who looked upon the imam as the highest legal authority were vehemently opposed to the casting of the imam in the role of gnostic savior. What concerned them particularly was that the gnostics were inclined to dismiss the religious law as irrelevant to the attainment of salvation. Although in Imamism belief in the imams was deemed to be essential for salvation, this was not a spiritualist doctrine. It was, rather, part of the belief that salvation was through the law and the only true version of the law was that transmitted by the imams.

The legalist scholars were also opposed to any conception of the imam that could undermine the belief in the cessation of prophecy after Muhammad or that entailed a belief in the possibility of incarnation. Furthermore, and as far as we can tell, early Shi'i gnostic doctrines focused on a single imam/savior figure and did not include recognition of the Imami principle of a permanent imamate or continuous line of imams. (The gnostics would single out one of the Imami or other 'Alid imams and cast him as a prophet or divine incarnation and the source of all the esoteric and saving knowledge in their hands.) This too would have been unacceptable to the Imami legalists. They labeled the gnostics as "exaggerators" (*ghulat*) and responded to the threat of their appeal by writing and publishing refutations of their doctrines.

The war that Imami legalists waged on the gnostic currents was, by and large, successful. It was successful in that gnostic concepts of salvation did not become part of Imami doctrine, and the emphasis remained on the authority of the law. However, by the end of the third/ninth century many other beliefs about the imams, which had previously been associated with Shi'i gnostics and messianists, began to appear (usually in modified form) in the Imami literature. This literature shows that the imams had come to be credited with a preexistence and an elevated spiritual status. Supernatural knowledge and an ability to perform miracles were also attributed to them. Older and much more moderate ideas about their role, knowledge, and nature were almost completely overshadowed. (With regard to the modern scholarly debates concerning the nature of early Imamism and the course of its development, referred to in the Preface, the other two main views, which differ from the one followed here and elsewhere in this book, may be mentioned: that esoteric/gnostic currents existed within early Imamism and influenced its conception of the imamate from the beginning; and (a more recent view) that Imamism originated as an esoteric doctrine and began to shed this legacy after the disappearance of the twelfth imam and under the influence of scholars whose interests were mainly in law and theology.)

As for the gnostics, they were more successful in propagating their teachings and their doctrine of salvation away from the main centers of Imami learning, from which they were gradually pushed out. Their separateness from Imamism was reflected in their adoption of variant lines of imams and non-Imami imams for their savior figures and, as in the case of the early Isma'ilis, in their espousal of an ideology of messianic activism.

The Occultation of the Twelfth Imam

Another doctrine that had been associated with non-Imami Shi'is and was adopted by Imamis in the later third/ninth century was the doctrine of occultation and return of the Mahdi. As we have said, this doctrine had its origins among messianic Shi'i groups. It had also been adopted by Imami splinter groups who decided that the line of imams had come to an end and applied the doctrine to the seventh imam whom they regarded as the last of the line. Sometime after the death of the eleventh imam, the Imami leadership announced that he had been succeeded by a young son and that the latter was now in hiding due to the threat to his life from the ruling authorities. Those who disagreed and voiced other views about the identity and/or role of the next imam (the sources report twelve or fourteen such groups) were portrayed as deviant. At first it was implied that his absence was going to be temporary and his return as the Mahdi within his lifetime. But gradually this became an event which would take place at the end of time.

Modern historians have related the adoption by Imamism of the doctrine of the Mahdi to the atmosphere of revolt and heightened messianic expectations, which prevailed at that time. The Imami leaders themselves had an interest in stable government and were opposed to revolt. A number of them were employed at court and in the administration as secretaries and even viziers, and acted as patrons and protectors to scholars. But many of their followers would have been attracted to the idea of their imam as the awaited Mahdi and perhaps even eager to engage in action on his behalf. In those circumstances the leadership could not afford to be seen as failing to support the imam. The idea of a hidden imam/Mahdi whose appearance could be postponed indefinitely would have seemed to be a good solution, especially when coupled, as it was, with the stipulation that any political action in his absence and without his openly declared consent was unlawful.

At first it was suggested that the hidden imam was in touch with his community through a number of trusted disciples. But the situation was exploited by extremist leaders who could now claim that they were conveying the wishes and teachings of the imam without the threat of being denounced by the imam himself. The moderate leadership in Baghdad responded by declaring that contact between the imam and his community had been taking place strictly through a series of sole representatives or mediators (*safirs*) and by recognizing one of their number as the current mediator. But the leadership could not continue to support the claims of its chosen mediators, especially at a time when doubts were being raised about the continued existence of the imam beyond a natural lifespan. Thus, the institution was abandoned and the idea that gained most acceptance among scholars was that the imam had passed into a "greater occultation" and that all communication with him had come to an end in the year 329/941. The idea suggests that it was by now clear to leaders and scholars, though perhaps not to the rank and file, that his absence would be permanent.

Another factor in the adoption of the doctrine of the occulted Mahdi may have been a gradual erosion of the status of the imamate. The sources report that after the death of each imam there were disagreements about the identity of his successor. The claims of an imam were often contested by a brother or an uncle. Two of the imams were minors when their fathers died, which led to all sorts of theoretical problems. For example, some Imamis questioned whether obedience to a minor was possible. Others said that the accession of a minor invalidates the belief in the perfect transmission of the Prophet's legacy. Moreover, Imami scholars had already emerged as, or perhaps they had always been, the actual religious leaders in their local communities, in which case the transition to living without an imam would not have been so difficult.

The difficulty lay in how to explain this turnaround, from Imamism to Twelverism; from insisting on the necessity of having an imam at all times to recognition that the imam of the time was absent and out of the reach of ordinary mortals; from the belief that he will lead the community as the Mahdi and redresser of injustices in the near future and that other imams will succeed him to the belief that he was the last of the line and that his appearance will be at the end of time. The changes produced confusion in the minds of the believers and doubts about the existence of the imam. Imami scholars spoke of this period in their history as the period of "perplexity" and they devised a number of arguments in order to justify the occultation and its prolongation. But although eventually the believers were convinced, outsiders continued to attack Imamis for what they saw as an intrinsic contradiction in their doctrine: the necessity of the imamate, and the occultation of the imam of the time, or how an imam whose role as guide was deemed to be necessary can ever be absent. Imami treatises devoted to the justification of the occultation were still being written well into the fifth/eleventh century. As we shall see, Mufid made significant contributions to this debate.

Imami Literature

Everything we know about early Imamism comes from the writings of its scholars and from reports about their views and the debates they conducted with other Muslims. The imams themselves are unlikely to have left behind any writings. (The ascription to them of a number of extant Imami works is unlikely to be genuine and was sometimes contested within Imamism itself.) Moreover, there is no reliable way of assessing the authenticity of the large body of Imami Hadith, the orally transmitted statements of the imams and reports about them believed by Imamis to preserve their actual words and teachings. The extent of the imams' contribution to the emergence and development of Imami doctrine is, thus, difficult to determine.

The literature that was produced by scholars before the occultation consisted mostly of short treatises which dealt with single topics of law or dogma, especially those disputed between Imamis and their opponents. There were also polemical treatises against other Shiʻi and non-Shiʻi sects. Most of this literature is not extant. We know something about it from quotations in later works and from the bibliographical dictionaries that were produced by later Imamis. A partial explanation as to why it did not survive is that in view of the major changes that Imamism underwent, much of the writings of earlier scholars would have become redundant; they either ceased to be copied, or were incorporated into later works, after being modified and updated.

The literature that appeared between the end of third/ninth century and the middle of the fourth/tenth was devoted to the definition, defense, and propagation of Twelver Imami doctrine. In addition to works on the imamate and the occultation, it included heresiographies (works on Islamic "sects and doctrines") and polemical treatises against other Shi'is. The heresiographers described divisions in Shi'ism up to the time of the twelfth imam and presented them as deviations from an original doctrine, which they deemed to be identical with Imamism and in existence since the time of the Prophet and 'Ali. (As must be clear by now, such presentations reflected a traditional view of authority, not historical reality.) They also described the current divisions that existed among Imamis over the identity and role of the twelfth imam, including the position of their own sect, the Imamiyya.

But the most authoritative works were the collections of Imami Hadith, deemed by Imamis to be the only true representation of the Sunna of the Prophet. One of the earliest collections, which is still regarded as one of four authoritative Imami collections, is that entitled "The Sufficient [Work] in the Science of Religion" by Muhammad ibn Ya'qub al-Kulini (d. 329/941). It was arranged according to the usual order of topics found in Sunni works of jurisprudence and Hadith. In addition to chapters on ritual purity, prayer, marriage, divorce, pilgrimage, and so on, which parallel those in Sunni works, it included a chapter on theology ("divine unity") and a long chapter on the imamate. It was put together in Baghdad and was said to have taken twenty years to complete. Much of its material was collected from narrators of Hadith from the Iranian city of Qumm, which had been a Shi'i center since the early Islamic period and growing in importance as a center of Imami learning during the third/ninth century.

Traditionalism and Rationalism

As its title indicates, Kulini's Hadith collection was intended as a complete record of the laws, dogmas, and ethical teachings of Imamism. It reflected the traditionalist attitude that had been characteristic of early Imamism and was still prevalent in the period of the "lesser occultation." This attitude was based on the idea that the Islamic revelation, as taught by the imams, contained all the laws and dogmas that mankind needed, and that the task of the scholar was merely to *find* those laws and dogmas from the corpus of Imami Hadith, not to *derive* or *formulate* new ones. Imami scholars maintained that juristic activity, as practised by Sunni and other scholars who believed themselves to be authorized to derive God's law from the Qur'an and Prophetic Hadith, was misguided, fallible, and superfluous.

This traditionalism became increasingly difficult to uphold after the onset of the "greater occultation" when all contact between the imam and his community was said to have come to an end. There soon began to appear attempts to admit a role for reason and interpretation. In the field of theology the use of reason provoked a negative reaction from Qummi scholars and their leading spokesman Abu Ja'far Muhammad ibn Babuya al-Qummi (d. 381/991), who was one of Mufid's teachers. But the rationalizing current that he was eager to arrest was to receive a boost at the hands of Mufid. The controversy between them on the role and legitimacy of theological inquiry and debate and the background to it will be discussed in Chapter 5.

In the legal sphere we witness the emergence of jurisprudence as an Imami discipline and a movement away from the idea that the transmitted body of Imami Hadith was a clear and sufficient expression of the law. The development generated debates and disputes within Imamism as to how, on what basis, and to what extent the scholars were authorized to define the law in the absence of the imam. Mufid's contribution to the development of jurisprudence will be discussed in Chapter 6.

2

THE TIMES AND CAREER
OF MUFID

Mufid was born in the year 336/948 in 'Ukbara, a town on
the Tigris river to the north of Baghdad. When he was
very young his father, who was a teacher, brought him with him
to Baghdad where he began his education. The city had been a
main center of Imamism since the late second/eighth century.
All the major developments in doctrine and in community
organization were closely associated with it: the formulation of
an Imami doctrine of the imamate, the defense of Imami legalism against messianic and gnostic currents, the adoption of the
doctrine of occultation of the twelfth imam, the concept of
sifara or representation of the twelfth imam during his "lesser
occultation" and its suspension, all were first expressed in liter-
ary form by scholars from, or closely associated with, Baghdad.
The major Imami Hadith collection of Kulini, which is recognized as the first of four authoritative collections, was put
together during twenty of the thirty years or so that he spent in
Baghdad.

Of course, there was much interchange between Imamis at
Baghdad and at other centers in Iraq and Iran, but Imami
scholars from other centers who had major contributions to
make would often end up living or spending time in Baghdad.
The attraction of Baghdad became even greater under the

exceptionally favorable conditions of rule by the Iranian dynasty of the Buyids.

THE BUYIDS

The Buyids came from a Zaydi Shiʻi background. They had risen to power in western Iran around the year 320/932 and soon extended their domains to include large parts of Iraq as well. Their arrival in Baghdad in 334/945 dealt another blow to the power of the ʻAbbasid caliphate, which had been in decline since the third/ninth century. In the provinces actual power had been in the hands of local dynasties of governors, and from 324/936 power in Baghdad lay in the hands of the army commander. Under the Buyids the caliph was deprived of a vizier and his influence was limited to making religious appointments for the Sunnis in Baghdad.

Though Shiʻis, the Buyids made no attempt to abolish the Sunni caliphate or to replace it with a Shiʻi one. They kept the caliph as nominal head of state and, like other independent dynasties that flourished in the fourth/tenth century, they exercised authority as his "appointed" governors. The caliph would grant them diplomas of investiture and confer on them titles indicating their role as guardians of the ʻAbbasid state. In their decision to keep the ʻAbbasid caliph the Buyids were undoubtedly influenced by the fact that the majority of their subjects, as well as the Turkish troops on whom they relied, were Sunnis. There were, in any case, problems facing any attempt to replace him with a ʻAlid caliph. The Imami imam had been in a state of occultation for almost seventy years, and the Imami leaders and scholars showed no readiness to accept change in the *status quo*. As for the Zaydi Shiʻis, they could have only accepted an ʻAlid who had laid claim to the caliphate and attempted to secure power for himself. And if the Buyids were to recognize the existing Fatimid 'Alid caliph who ruled over North Africa and (from 358/969) Egypt, this would have entailed submission to the authority of someone who wielded considerable political and military power – something which they were clearly not prepared to do.

Although from a Zaydi background, the Buyid rulers tended to sympathize also (and eventually more) with the Imamis. In fact, it is unclear whether they continued to adhere to Zaydism. There is evidence that some of them may have adopted Imamism. The second Buyid ruler in Baghdad, the amir Mu'izz al-Dawla (d. 356/967), was buried near the graves of Imami imams. 'Adud al-Dawla (d. 372/983), the most outstanding of all the Buyid amirs, who reigned in Shiraz and later in Baghdad, appears to have been devoted to the twelve imams, as is attested from an inscription of his which lists their names along with blessings. This leaning towards Imamism may have had something to do with the fact that, with its quietism and doctrine of a hidden imam, it was compatible with the Buyid requirement of independence in government, whereas Zaydism, with its history and ideology of activism, held a potential challenge to the legitimacy of their rule.

IMAMISM UNDER THE BUYIDS

In any case, from the moment of their accession to power the Buyids took measures and pursued policies aimed at safeguarding and promoting Shi'i interests and ensuring that Shi'is had the freedom to practise their rituals openly and to express their religious beliefs and sentiments. Under their protective rule, Shi'i communities and Shi'i learning flourished. In Iraq, where most of the Shi'is were Imamis, Imami scholars received

patronage from the amirs and viziers of the Buyid establishment. In 352/963, under Mu'izz al-Dawla, two Imami festivals
were established as official celebrations. The festival of
'Ashura', commemorating the martyrdom of 'Ali's son
Husayn, killed at Karbala' in 61/680 when he rose against the
Umayyads, was celebrated openly with public mourning. The
events known as Ghadir Khumm, when the Prophet was said to
have designated 'Ali as his successor, were celebrated at another
festival. The Buyid rulers also protected and extended the
shrines of the imams, which were becoming increasingly
important as places of Imami pilgrimage.

In 381/991 the pro-Shi'i vizier Shapur ibn Ardashir founded
the Dar al-'Ilm (House of Learning) in Karkh, the Shi'i quarter
of Baghdad where Mufid lived and worked. The establishment
is said to have housed a library of a hundred thousand volumes.
There are also references to boarding facilities for students.
Much of the canonical Hadith literature of the Imamiyya was
produced in this period, as was the literature in which the dogmatic positions of the sect were elaborated and defended and to
which Mufid made significant contributions.

Shi'ism also benefited from the close relations between local
families of 'Alid descent and the Buyid court. The 'Alids, who
could lay claim to the title of *sayyid* (lord) or *sharif* (nobleman),
had been emerging as a revered social group and had certain
privileges, such as entitlement to special pensions from the
state. They were organized under the leadership of their own
head (*naqib*) who received his appointment from the ruler. The
naqib was responsible for the family tree and making sure that
no false claimants were allowed to pass as 'Alids. He was also
responsible for the distribution of pensions and the administration of justice within the group and between 'Alids and non-
'Alids. According to some modern scholars, it was the Buyids
who gave the 'Alids this organization and made it similar to, and

independent of, that of the 'Abbasid Hashimites. Others, however, have traced this organization and the institution of the 'Alid *naqib* to the late third/ninth century. Be that as it may, it is clear that under the Buyids the 'Alids became increasingly influential, both socially and politically. Some of their families became hereditary guardians of the shrines of the imams. Leading 'Alids were involved in the settlement of internal disputes and were sent as emissaries to foreign powers such as Byzantium and the Fatimids. A number of them occupied themselves with religious scholarship. Some were inclined to Zaydism, others to Imamism, but there were also some Sunnis among them.

At first the Buyids tended to favor the Zaydis in their appointment of the 'Alid *naqib* in Baghdad. But from 353/964, and for nearly a century, the office came to be occupied by the Imami Abu Ahmad al-Musawi (though in his case, not continuously, as he was several times removed), and his two sons Radi (d. 406/1015) and Murtada (d. 436/1044). Mufid was closely connected to this family. He was chosen as educator to the two brothers. Both became distinguished poets and scholars. Murtada left important writings in theology and law and succeeded Mufid as leader of the Imamiyya. Radi is associated with the composition of *Nahj al-balagha* ("The Path of Rhetoric"), a large work which consists of collected sermons and sayings ascribed to the imam 'Ali.

OTHER RELIGIOUS GROUPS

That is not to say that under the Buyids Shi'ism flourished at the expense of other religious groups. Buyid rule was tolerant and enlightened, and under it the Islamic world experienced a cultural efflorescence and transformation unparalleled in earlier or later times. Although the Buyids were proud of their Iranian origins, and in fact presented themselves as Persian rulers, they were not interested in the revival of Persian culture and soon assimilated themselves to Arabic culture. The rulers and their viziers played an important role as patrons of Arabic and Islamic learning and helped create an atmosphere that was conducive to the free flow and exchange of ideas. Their courts in Baghdad, Rayy, and Shiraz were centers for the patronage of distinguished poets, religious scholars from various schools and sects, and other men of learning. Debating sessions (*majalis*) were held there in which representatives from the various religious groups took part, and where it was common to find non-Muslims among the participants. The debates were at a high level of learning. According to the account of an Andalusian visitor to Baghdad in the late fourth/tenth century, the rules prohibited reliance on the authority of revelation and participants had to argue strictly from reason.

The Mu'tazila and Other Theologians

Mu'tazilism, the leading school of rationalist theology in early Islam and a main contributor to the process of hellenization of Islamic thought, had been shifting to Iran since the late third/ninth century, as it had to contend with the hostility of the caliphs and their supporters among the traditionists, the Hadith scholars, who were strongly represented in Iraq. Under the Buyids it acquired new vigor. Its two rival schools, known (after the places of origin of their founders) as the Basran and the Baghdadian Mu'tazila, were represented in Baghdad in our period. Leading Mu'tazili personalities received patronage from Buyid viziers and were appointed to senior positions in the administration. The distinguished scholar and judge, 'Abd al-Jabbar (d. 415/1025), of the Basran school lived and worked in Baghdad for a time, and later enjoyed a long career as chief judge in Rayy (near modern-day Tehran) at the court of the Buyid vizier Sahib ibn 'Abbad, himself a Mu'tazili.

In Baghdad, Sunni scholars of the Hanafi school of law were attracted to Mu'tazili theology. Other Sunnis favored Ash'ari theology. Its founder, Abu al-Hasan al-Ash'ari (d. 324/935), had adopted some of the rationalist methods of the Mu'tazila and used them to formulate and defend traditionalist dogma. In our period its most famous spokesman was the Sunni jurist and judge Baqillani (d. 403/1013). An encounter between him and Mufid over the question of the imamate has been documented.

But Mu'tazili thought exerted a far greater and more permanent influence on Shi'ism than on Sunnism. In Zaydi Shi'ism, which had been receptive to Mu'tazili influence since the middle of the third/ninth century, the late fourth/tenth century was a high point in the process of integration of Mu'tazili theology. Imami Shi'ism also became more open to Mu'tazili influence, although its doctrine of the imamate acted as a doctrinal barrier against a more thorough integration. As we shall see, Mufid played a key role in steering Imamism towards a more rational theology and the position he took on a number of questions reflects Mu'tazili influence.

The Sunnis

The Buyids in Iraq, as elsewhere, tried to be even-handed in their treatment of the communities and at times would go to great lengths to show goodwill towards Sunnism. Nevertheless, some of their pro-Shi'i policies contributed to communal tensions. The conflicts between Shi'is and Sunnis, which had their roots in an earlier period, resurfaced, and armed confrontations became increasingly violent and frequent, especially around the time of the religious festivals. (In 389/999 two Sunni festivals, designed to rival the Shiʻi ones that Muʻizz al-Dawla had established in 352/963, began to be celebrated.) On three occasions Mufid was banished from Baghdad by the Buyid authorities, although there is no evidence that he was personally involved in igniting the riots, and he was always allowed to return.

Sunnism was defined not by dogmatic positions but increasingly by adherence to one of the main legal *madhhab*s or schools of jurisprudence. It was during the fourth/tenth century that four of them, each with a legal tradition going back (or ascribed) to an eponymous founder, came to be regarded as "orthodox." The schools were united by their common acceptance of the sources of the law, and the fact that there were differences among them regarding the details or substance of the law was justified on the basis of divine sanction.

The Sunni scholars who were at the forefront of opposition to the growing influence of Shiʻism were of the Hanbali legal rite. The Hanbalis had wide popular appeal and militant tendencies had appeared among them. Like other Sunnis, the Hanbalis had come to recognize ʻAli as one of the four rightly guided caliphs of Islam, but against the Shiʻi view of ʻAli as the only legitimate caliph they promoted the superiority of the first three. Also particularly objectionable from their point of view was the Imami rejection of the Prophetic tradition as transmitted from the Prophet's companions.

The Hanbalis were also strict traditionalists and resented the influence that Muʻtazili rationalism was exerting on Islamic thought. Although, like the other schools of law, they had come to accept an element of reasoning in the derivation of law from the revealed sources, in matters of dogma they remained opposed to the use of reason. In the later Buyid period, when Buyid power was on the decline, the traditionalist cause was strengthened by the actions of the caliph Qadir (r. 381/ 991–422/1031). The latter took a series of measures aimed at

reasserting the authority of the caliphate, which were presented as upholding and protecting traditionalist Sunni values.

The first sign that something like this was taking place was in
394/1003 when the caliph refused to recognize the appointment by the Buyid amir, Baha' al-Dawla, of the head of the 'Alid
family, the *naqib*, as chief judge. In 408/1017 he issued a decree
prohibiting discussion of Shi'i and Mu'tazili doctrines. Sunni
Hanafi jurists, many of whom were sympathetic to Mu'tazili
theology, were obliged to disavow those doctrines publicly; if
they refused, they would be banned from holding office as
judges and official witnesses. In 409/1018 he proclaimed a
profession of faith which served to define the official dogma of
the state. Further proclamations were given in 420/1029. This
Qadiri creed, as it came to be known, supported the position of
the Hanbali traditionalists and denounced many of the doctrines held by the Mu'tazilis, Imamis, Ash'aris, and Isma'ili
Shi'is. One of the points emphasized was the duty of all
Muslims to venerate the companions of the Prophet, which
was a sore point for the Shi'is and especially the Imamis among
them. Mufid defended the Imami position concerning the
Prophet's companions in a number of his writings.

The Isma'ilis

In the first part of their reign (down to c. 370/980) the Buyids
had to deal with the potential threat to their power and authority from Isma'ili Shi'ism. Isma'ilism began as a messianic movement that preached the advent of the 'Alid Mahdi. It achieved
political success when the Fatimids, a 'Alid dynasty, came to
power in North Africa and from 358/969 went on to conquer
and rule from Egypt. The Fatimids traced their descent to a different branch of the 'Alid family from the one recognized by the
Imami Shi'is. They claimed to be the sole legitimate rulers of

the Islamic community and, in line with this claim, they did not abandon their missionary activities when they came to power.

However, a territorial threat from the Fatimids to Buyid domains never materialized. A major reason for this were the ongoing hostilities between them and the Byzantines and the fact that they stood to benefit from reaching an agreement with the Buyids and making common cause with them against the Byzantines.

Another Isma'ili state, that of the Qaramita, was found in Bahrain. The Qaramita did not recognize the Fatimids as legitimate rulers and continued to adhere to the original messianic doctrine. They launched attacks on Fatimid territories in Egypt, Syria, and Palestine, and rejected the calls of the Fatimid caliphs to pay them allegiance. They also acted against the Buyids by attacking southern Iraq. The Buyids managed to keep them at bay by giving them land grants and inviting them to send an envoy to Bahgdad. Their threat receded after 378/988 when they were defeated by a local ruler from southern Iraq.

Fatimid Isma'ilism presented an ideological challenge to Imamism. The Fatimid caliphs laid claim to, and were recognized by their Isma'ili followers as, supreme religious authority over the whole of the Muslim community. The doctrine preached by their missionary organization (da'wa) was attractive to other Shi'is, including many intellectuals. Some Shi'is of Iraq were attracted to the Fatimid court in Cairo. In 398/1007, during unrest in Baghdad, the Shi'i crowd called out the name of the Fatimid caliph Hakim, calling him "Mansur" (Victorious), a messianic title. In 401/1010 the ruler of Mosul, Kufa, and other Iraqi towns acknowledged the suzerainty of the Fatimid caliph, and other local chiefs followed suit.

The Buyid rulers appear to have tolerated the activities of Fatimid missionaries who operated in several towns of Iraq and western Iran. They also appear to have been prepared to recognize the Fatimids as members of the *ahl al-bayt* (the Prophet's Family) and to exonerate them from the charge of having falsified their 'Alid genealogy.

But despite the ideological challenge from Fatimid Isma'ilism, Imami scholars in Buyid Baghdad appear to have made little attempt to deal with it in their writings. This is difficult to explain. Perhaps they did not wish to antagonize ordinary Imamis who, because of the conditions of intense sectarian strife that prevailed in Iraq, were inclined to look to the Fatimid rulers as a potential source of help in their struggle against their Sunni opponents. Perhaps they felt secure in the knowledge that the Buyid rulers would never recognize the spiritual authority of the Fatimids and would continue to protect Imamism. In any case, Imamis appear to have been content to let others campaign against Fatimid legitimacy and refute Isma'ili doctrine. After the Fatimid conquest of Egypt and the move of the caliph to Cairo, the question of Fatimid ancestry was reopened. Sometime after 373/983 a Damascene 'Alid by the name of Akhu Muhsin wrote a hostile account of the rise of the Fatimids and accused them of having falsified their genealogy. In 402/1011 the 'Abbasid caliph Qadir assembled a number of scholars and notables and commanded them to declare in a written document that the Fatimid caliph Hakim and his predecessors lacked genuine 'Alid ancestry. The document was signed by Imamis, including Mufid, Radi, and Murtada.

THE CAREER OF MUFID

Mufid received his education and spent all his working life in Baghdad. He studied under prominent Imami scholars. His teacher in theology was Abu al-Jaysh al-Muzaffar al-Balkhi (d. 367/977), who was the spokesman of the Imamiyya and a leading theologian. In jurisprudence and Hadith Mufid received instruction from a number of Qummi scholars who had settled in Baghdad or traveled and taught there for a time during his years of education; the most notable among them were Ja'far ibn Quluya (d. 368/978), with whom Mufid studied Kulini's *Kafi* ("The Sufficient"), and Ibn Babuya, who was the compiler of the second great collection of Imami Hadith.

Mufid became well acquainted with the doctrines of the other schools and sects and distinguished himself as a skilled debater. He was soon (probably after the death of his teacher Abu al-Jaysh, but before the death of his other teacher, Ibn Babuya) recognized as the leading spokesman of the Imamiyya, a position that he held until his death. The atmosphere in Baghdad was one of intense intellectual vitality and character-ized by frequent polemical encounters between members of the various religious groups. Mufid was very much part of that atmosphere. He attended debating sessions, and held some in his own house and the mosque he had built next to it, which were open to all scholars. The amir 'Adud al-Dawla is said to have visited him often and sometimes attended those sessions. There are numerous reports of Mufid's disputes with Mu'tazili and Sunni scholars, among those mentioned are the Mu'tazilis 'Abd al-Jabbar and Rummani, and the Sunni Ash'ari Baqillani. The list of his works, which comes close to two hundred (most of which are known to us only by their titles), includes several refutations (*radd*) of the views and treatises of Mu'tazilis, Zaydis, and Sunnis.

The importance of those encounters in the formation of Mufid's thought cannot be over-emphasized. In fact, the polemical impulse characterizes much of his work. Many, if not most, of his listed works are on topics of dispute between Imamis and their opponents. And as his extant works show, when formulating his juristic and theological arguments he would not only build on (and, in a few cases, reject) existing Imami positions and beliefs. He would often also delineate the points of difference between Imamism and its opponents.

Closely related to this polemical impulse was a desire on the part of Mufid to define Imamism along more rationalist lines. He realized the importance of the use of reason in defending the beliefs and historical claims of Imamism and in the elaboration of distinctive theological positions. But his advocacy of reason was combined with an insistence on the status of revelation (i.e., the Qur'an and Hadith) as the main source in theology and law. In this he departed from the strict traditionalist position of his teacher, Ibn Babuya. Mufid felt strongly about the role of reason and he was confident enough of his own standing and authority to criticize openly his teacher's negative attitude to rationalist theology (kalam) and to write a "correction" (tashih) of his dogma. His efforts in this regard opened the way for the greater rationalization of Imamism that took place at the hands of his pupils, Murtada and Shaykh Abu Ja'far Muhammad al-Tusi (d. 460/1067) and subsequent generations of Imami scholars.

The fact that his authority was widely recognized is reflected in the large number of his written answers (jawabat) to questions addressed to him by Imamis from all over the Islamic world, and in his composition of a number of works entitled "epitome," which dealt with single topics of law or dogma and were intended as a means of instructing the faithful in the right doctrine and practice.

Mufid died on the second of Ramadan (29 November) in 413/1022. His funeral is said to have been attended by a huge crowd (eighty thousand mourners, according to one source). It was usual for distinguished Imamis to be buried near the shrines of the imams, and Mufid was buried in Baghdad near the shrines of the seventh and ninth imams, Musa al-Kazim and Muhammad al-Jawad.

3

THE IMAMATE: THE
HISTORICAL ARGUMENTS

The classical Imami conception of the imamate as it appeared in the literature that emerged after the occultation at the turn of the third/ninth century was a composite one, and the product of complex development. It incorporated the views of scholars whose outlook was essentially legalistic and whose interests were mainly in the traditional religious sciences, as well as elements rooted in messianic and gnostic thought and aspects of popular piety.

The picture that emerges from that literature is that of imams endowed with superhuman qualities. The twelve imams were prophets in all but name, and belief in them was essential for the attainment of salvation. The only difference between them and the Prophet (or any other messenger prophet) was that they did not bring forth a divine law or transmit a scripture, and they were not entitled to abrogate any of the precepts revealed to him. The imams were entitled to rule as caliphs but their religious authority did not depend on actual rule or on any attempt to gain it. They were infallible (*ma'sum*) in all their acts and decisions. They were distinguished from the rest of mankind by their special knowledge (*'ilm*) and access to divine inspiration (*ilham*). The designation (*nass*) of each imam by his predecessor was deemed to have been an expression of the divine will and to have begun with the Prophet's designation of 'Ali as his successor. The presence of the imams as Proofs (*hujja*) of the divine will is essential for guidance and even for the continued existence of the world. The belief that the earth can never be devoid of one of God's Proofs appears at an early stage as an argument in support of the existence of the twelfth imam in a state of earthly occultation.

The Imami imamate was not just the focus of community devotion and the object of pious speculation. It was also believed to be the source of all the religious knowledge in the hands of scholars and others of its adherents. The imams were believed to have acted as teachers and interpreters of the revealed law and passed on to their followers all the heritage of the Prophet. With the severance of contact between the hidden imam and his community, the guidance that the imams had provided did not come to an end. It could still be sought in the corpus of Hadith transmitted from them. That corpus was thought to embody all the knowledge that mankind needed for its religion. Because this knowledge came from infallible imams, it was superior to and more authoritative than the knowledge in the hands of other Muslims who received it from ordinary and hence fallible transmitters. There was, therefore, much at stake in defending the imamate. The role of the Imami scholar as a religious leader and his claim to be in possession of authoritative knowledge rested on it.

Mufid used two approaches in his treament and defense of the Imami imamate: the historical/hagiographical and the rational/theological. This chapter is concerned with his contribution to the former.

He was not the first Imami scholar to collect traditions on the lives of the imams, and many of the traditions he included had appeared in earlier works. Moreover, the material he collected does not add up to comprehensive biographies in the style of *sira* or "life" of the Prophet. Rather, it consisted mainly of individual reports that dealt with various aspects of an imam's life and career, his credentials, his perfect knowledge, his miracles, and so forth. But Mufid went further than any of his predecessors in his attempt to prove the validity of the Imami imamate by arguments based on the historical sources. He made extensive, though clearly selective, use of the mainstream (viz. the Sunni-oriented) historical tradition, especially when dealing with the imamate of 'Ali. His accounts were essentially apologetic and served to show the imams as having interacted with the authorities, with other 'Alid claimants, and with their own followers in ways commensurate with their status and role as Imami imams. But his accounts also served a polemical purpose in that a good part of his material reflected the Imami response to objections and criticisms by opponents. In order to understand the significance of this material in Imamism and to appreciate Mufid's contribution, a word must be said about the historical tradition on early Islam.

THE MAINSTREAM HISTORICAL TRADITION

The historical tradition began to take shape and to be written down by religious scholars before the emergence of Imami and Zaydi Shi'ism in the late second/eighth century. There was much sympathy for 'Ali and his descendants among those scholars. This is reflected in some of the accounts concerning 'Alids who rose against the existing rulers and were brutally crushed, but mostly in reports and material concerning the role played by 'Ali during the time of the Prophet and first three caliphs and during his own career as fourth caliph. By the third/ninth century, however, Islamic historiography was beginning to be dominated by mainstream scholars, the future Sunnis. Most of those scholars were now inclined to venerate 'Ali as one of four rightly guided caliphs (all four had been companions of the Prophet and ruled over the community founded by him in Medina), but they rejected the Shi'i view that only 'Ali and his successors were entitled to the caliphate and had a special ability to guide the community in religious matters. The Sunni scholars regarded themselves, and not the caliphs or anyone else, as the religious guides of the community, and were suspicious of any claims to religious leadership that seemed to undermine their own authority. They were also becoming increasingly quietist and looked unfavorably upon any idea which seemed to challenge the political authority of the 'Abbasid caliphs and any claim to political power that threatened to bring about change in the *status quo*.

The Imamis, who at that time were beginning to develop their own tradition about the lives of 'Ali and his successors, adopted the view that the first caliphs and most of the early community had erred and disobeyed the Prophet's explicit instructions when they failed to recognize 'Ali as imam after the Prophet's death. The Imamis, therefore, were not in a position to influence or to contribute to the mainstream historical tradition. Consequently, there is not much in that tradition as it stands that could support the Imami conception of the imamate.

Nevertheless, from the time of their emergence the Imamis (and the Zaydi Shi'is) would make use of the pro-'Ali reports found in the mainstream tradition and interpret them in ways that supported their own beliefs concerning his imamate and his designation by the Prophet. Their opponents also would adduce reports and events from that tradition when trying to refute those interpretations. Opponents would argue, for example, that had the Prophet had any intention to designate a successor he would have made it known to all Muslims and would have been explicit about it. Another favorite and enduring argument by opponents was that 'Ali was not known to have contested the accession of the first three caliphs who preceded him, and he even gave them the oath of allegiance. This, they said, would not have happened had 'Ali believed himself to have been the Prophet's intended successor.

Opponents would also argue that well known and widely reported events and information about other 'Alids recognized by Imamis as imams do not support the Imami view of things. Those 'Alids, they would say, acted in ways not compatible with a view of themselves as Imami imams or with the claim of their followers that they were infallible. In the time of Mufid a main criticism was that the reports about their imams were transmitted by few witnesses and only within Imamism, and therefore did not meet the criteria of authenticity or count as valid proofs of the Imami imamate.

Mufid's extant works on the imams show that he attached much importance to tackling this kind of anti-Imami polemic. His *Book of Guidance (Kitab al-Irshad)* is recognized by Imamis as one of the most important works of its kind. In it Mufid deals with the issues surrounding the imamate of each of the twelve imams and, most extensively, with those of the imamate of 'Ali.

THE IMAMATE OF 'ALI

Concerning 'Ali, Mufid sought to prove from the life story (*sira*) of the Prophet and the history of the early caliphate that 'Ali was the most excellent of the Prophet's companions and was designated by him to be his successor. He often says of the accounts he gives that they are well known from all works of *sira*, that they have been narrated by both Shi'is and Sunnis, or that the transmitters of reports are all agreed on the events. Although Mufid does not always name his sources, many of the accounts he cites are in fact recognizable from the mainstream *sira* tradition and have many elements in common with it. But they also have significant variations and additional details and interpretations, which are distinctly Imami in provenance and purpose. In fact, 'Ali plays a much bigger role in those accounts than he does in the Sunni *sira* and other sources.

'Ali as the Most Excellent Companion of the Prophet

By the fourth/tenth century all Sunni and Mu'tazili Muslims had come to regard 'Ali as one of four rightly guided caliphs; the other three, in chronological order, were Abu Bakr, 'Umar, and 'Uthman. They remained opposed to the Shi'i view that 'Ali had the sole right to succeed the Prophet and highly critical of the Shi'i repudiation of the caliphates of the other three. Against the Shi'i view that 'Ali was the most excellent of the Prophet's companions and that he had the sole right to succeed him, there developed among Sunnis and Mu'tazilis mainly two views as to how 'Ali and the other three caliphs ranked in the matter of merit and whether the rightful imamate was restricted to "the most excellent" (*al-afdal*) member of the community. Most said that it was, and that each of the first four caliphs was "the most excellent" when he acceded to the caliphate. In other words, they ranked 'Ali as fourth in excellence at the time of the Prophet's death. Some of the Mu'tazila said that 'Ali was the most excellent of men *after the death of the Prophet*, meaning that he was more excellent than the other three caliphs who preceded him, but that the imamates of "the less excellent" (that is, of the three caliphs) were also legitimate.

For Mufid and the Imamis neither of these two positions was acceptable. They regarded 'Ali as the most excellent

companion of the Prophet and entitled to succeed him imme-
diately after his death; it followed that the imamates of the first
three caliphs were not legitimate. Mufid sought to provide
elaborate proof for the Imami position from the mainstream
historical tradition. The accounts he gives in his *Book of Guidance*
deal with 'Ali's heroic deeds, his closeness to the Prophet, and
his contributions to the early Islamic state. He highlights 'Ali's
role in *jihad* (holy war) and shows how he distinguished himself
in battles against the pagan Meccans and played a prominent
role in the subjugation of Arabia. His accounts include several
stories of 'Ali's miracles and knowledge of the unseen.

As part of his attempt to prove 'Ali's excellence, Mufid
defended the Imami position regarding the error of the companions of the Prophet and, especially, the three caliphs who
preceded 'Ali. The Imami position often came under attack
from other Muslims who countered it with their own arguments, proof texts, and Qur'anic interpretations and sought to
prove that the companions could not have conspired or acted
unlawfully against 'Ali. The Sunnis presented the companions
as men of virtue, to whom the Qur'an has promised forgive-
ness and eternal bliss in the Garden and whom the Prophet had
praised as "guiding stars." As regards the three caliphs, they
highlighted their virtues, their closeness to the Prophet, and
their role in holy war and other services to Islam, and made
much of the fact that they had acceded to the caliphate with the
support of leading Muslims.

Against the Sunni view, Mufid pointed to reports about
companions who apostatized from Islam after the death of the
Prophet and others who violated the oath of allegiance they had
given to 'Ali as caliph. He also tried to show that whilst there is
good evidence to suggest that those who supported the accession of 'Ali's predecessors stood to benefit from it, there is lack
of evidence that those predecessors were deserving of the

caliphate or that they had the virtues and qualities ascribed to them by Sunnis.

The Prophet's Designation of 'Ali at Ghadir Khumm

A good illustration of Mufid's historical approach to the question of the imamate may be found in the account he gives of an episode in the life of the Prophet, known (after its place of occurrence) as Ghadir Khumm (the spring of Khumm). The episode was regarded by Imamis (and by other early Shi'is) as one of the main foundation events in the history of their community.

The details of the event are found in numerous Hadith reports preserved in the Sunni collections. They may be summarized as follows. A few months before his death in 11/632 the Prophet, accompanied by 'Ali and a group of pilgrims, was on his way back to Medina from his "Farewell" pilgrimage to Mecca (so called because the address he gave there was regarded as marking the culminating point of his career), when he halted near the spring of Khumm. There he took 'Ali by the hand and gave an address to the gathered pilgrims. First he asked them to confirm that he, Muhammad, was closer (*awla*) to them than they were to themselves, which they did. He then declared: "All those whose *mawla* I am have 'Ali as their *mawla*." (The word has a wide range of meanings in Arabic. In this context the meaning could be either master or friend.) And according to some sources, the Prophet went on to say: "O God be the friend (*mawla*) of those who are his ('Ali's) friends and the enemy of those who are his enemies."

Most Sunni scholars accepted this report as authentic, and admitted it as proof of the duty of Muslims to venerate the Prophet's Family. But they refused to accept it as the basis of Shi'i claims regarding the 'Alid imamate. In some Sunni sources the episode is said to have been prompted by a dispute about the distribution of booty between 'Ali and the men who had accompanied him on a recent expedition to Yemen. The dispute is said to have been resolved when the Prophet acted as arbiter and ruled in favor of 'Ali; his statement regarding 'Ali as his and the believers' *mawla* was meant as an exhortation to the believers to venerate 'Ali and hold him in affection, and to put an end to the gossip about him.

The Imamis interpreted the Ghadir Khumm episode differently. They said that the declaration by the Prophet amounted to an act of explicit designation and was one of several other indications that he gave to his followers of his intention for 'Ali to succeed him. And whereas the Sunnis interpreted the word *mawla* used by the Prophet as meaning a friend, the Imamis insisted it meant leader and master.

The Zaydi Shi'is, for their part, disagreed with the Imamis on this point, or at least this was their view in the fourth/tenth century. They had always insisted that the first three imams (i.e., 'Ali and his two sons, Hasan and Husayn) were designated by the Prophet. Now they were saying that this designation had been ambiguous and its intended meaning could be discovered only by investigation. This claim enabled the Zaydis to absolve the early community of the sin of disobeying the Prophet, something which the Imamis were not prepared to do. The Zaydi position explains why Mufid's account emphasizes not only the fact of 'Ali's designation but also that it had been explicit.

The Imamis also relied on their own interpretations of the Qur'an in order to support their version of the Ghadir Khumm event. In early Islam the work of interpreting the Qur'an included a tendency to relate its various pieces of revelation (its verses and passages) to specific events and incidents in the life of the Prophet. It also involved identifying people and places that are only alluded to in the Qur'an. In Imamism there developed a tendency to interpret verses and passages as having been revealed about 'Ali and his successors. Thus, in connection with the Ghadir Khumm episode, they said that when the Prophet told his followers to take 'Ali as their *mawla* he was acting upon a revelation (Q. 5: 67) ordering him to inform them of what had already been revealed to him on earlier occasions, which, according to the Shi'i interpretation, concerned 'Ali's designation. The Prophet, they said, had kept secret the divine order to designate 'Ali because he was waiting for the right moment when there would be no more opposition to 'Ali among his followers. Another Qur'anic verse (Q. 5: 3), which was recognized by all Muslims as marking the end of all divine communications to the Prophet, was said by Imamis to have been revealed to him on the day of Ghadir Khumm: "Today I have perfected your religion for you, and I have completed my blessing upon you, and I have approved Islam for your religion." Imamis interpreted the "perfection of religion" as a reference to the imamate of 'Ali.

In the time of Mufid these Imami interpretations of the Qur'an had already provoked polemical responses from other Muslims. These verses, it was argued, were revealed at the Farewell Pilgrimage and not at Ghadir Khumm. Another objection was that if the verses really concerned the designation of 'Ali, the Prophet would have made the announcement at the Pilgrimage when a larger crowd would have been assembled; there would have been no reason for him to wait until he reached Ghadir Khumm when many of the pilgrims would have already dispersed.

In his account of the episode Mufid tried to deal with all these issues. Apparently responding to an objection that the halt at Khumm was for water and pasture and not to make an announcement about 'Ali's designation, Mufid tells us that the place at Ghadir Khumm is *not* a place of water or pasture. The Prophet stopped there because he received the Qur'anic revelation (Q. 5: 67) ordering him to proclaim the designation of 'Ali. God would have known that once past Ghadir Khumm most of the pilgrims would have left and dispersed to their different destinations, and He would have wanted them to be assembled for the announcement so that the proof of 'Ali's imamate would be a strong one. The Prophet had received earlier revelations about 'Ali's designation but they did not include specific instructions about when to make the announcement. So he postponed it until he could be certain that the people would not oppose him in this. Moreover, on the orders of the Prophet, 'Ali received the congratulations of Muslims, including none other than the future caliph 'Umar, who addressed 'Ali with the title of "*amir* of the faithful." Thus no one could claim that the Prophet's declaration did not constitute an act of designation or that the designation was ambiguous.

Regarding the word *mawla*, used by the Prophet in the Ghadir Khumm reports, Mufid sought to demonstrate that it meant imam/leader and that this meaning was in accordance with the common usage of early Muslims. To that end he adduced poetry composed by (or, in some cases, attributed to) well-known Shi'i and other poets from Islamic history. (In the interpretation of the Qur'an and Hadith, the use of poetry in support of particular meanings was common among early Muslims.) Mufid cited lines said by Imamis to have been composed and recited on that occasion by the Prophet's poet, Hassan. In them Hassan refers to the Prophet as saying to 'Ali: "I am pleased with you as an imam to mankind."

In this, as in other aspects of the dispute over the question of the imamate, Mufid had to deal with criticism from Mu'tazili scholars who would assail his evidence and the bases of his arguments. Some insight into what he was up against and how he dealt with it may be gained from an account of a (real or imaginary) debating session between himself and a Mu'tazili on the Ghadir Khumm report and the meaning of the word *mawla*. The Mu'tazili apparently rejected the Imami argument based on the evidence of Hassan's poetry, saying that what Hassan reported as the words of the Prophet is not the same as what the Imamis themselves accepted as the actual words of the Prophet. Moreover, Hassan was known for his devotion to the first three caliphs, that is to say, he was a proto-Sunni. It would follow that the lines concerned are spurious. The Mu'tazili also rejected the evidence of Shi'i poetry on the basis of its partisan character.

In defense of his arguments, Mufid cites lines by poets who were not known for their Shi'ism, in which the word *mawla* is used in the sense of leader. As regards Hassan, Mufid says it is a logical possibility that before adopting Sunnism he had been a Shi'i; there is nothing to preclude it in the accounts of Hassan's encounters with the Prophet. In other words, there is no basis for his opponent's rejection of the authenticity of those lines.

'Ali's Knowledge of the Law

Mufid drew on the Sunni tradition in order to demonstrate that 'Ali had been the most reliable source of legal knowledge in his time. In the Sunni tradition 'Ali appears as an authority on the law and a transmitter of Prophetic Hadith, but he is one of several other companions of the Prophet who appear in this role. Some Sunni reports seem to portray him as having been more knowledgeable in legal matters than the other companions. They do not, however, envisage him, as Imami reports do, in the role of sole religious authority or as endowed with special knowledge and infallibility. In Imamism, where the imam's perfect knowledge of the law was a main constituent of its conception of the imamate, reports of that nature acquired a far greater significance and provided additional proof that 'Ali was distinguished by his exceptional knowledge and was therefore the rightful imam.

Mufid produced a collection of 'Ali's legal judgments and described the circumstances in which they were made. These show that whereas the three caliphs and other leading figures often failed to resolve difficult legal problems, 'Ali was always able to give the right decision. 'Ali was often consulted by the other caliphs who (mostly) accepted his decisions and acted upon them, which goes to show that they recognized the superiority of his knowledge and hence his right to the imamate, although they were reluctant to admit this openly or to allow him to exercise his right.

'Ali's Infallibility and the Errors of the Prophet's Companions

In disputes between Imamis and their opponents the internal conflicts which took place during 'Ali's time as caliph were relevant to two related issues: the infallibility of his actions and the error of his opponents.

The conflicts in question began with the murder of the third caliph 'Uthman and continued during 'Ali's period as caliph. They ended with his murder and the accession of Mu'awiya, the founder of the Umayyad dynasty, in 41 / 661. The events are known in the Muslim tradition as the *Fitna* (lit., trial, test) and in modern scholarship as the First Civil War in Islam. When 'Ali became caliph he faced opposition from individuals loyal to the murdered caliph 'Uthman, who objected to 'Ali's failure to hand over his killers and to avenge his blood. There were two major conflicts, the battle of the Camel in which 'Ali fought against an alliance of malcontents led by 'A'isha, the Prophet's widow, and two of the Prophet's prominent companions, Talha and Zubayr, and the battle of Siffin against the Syrians led by Mu'awiya.

These events were of great importance in internal Muslim controversies, as later generations came to define their sectarian identities with reference to their rights and wrongs. The issues that occupied them were whether 'Uthman had been unjustly murdered and whether 'Ali had been right in acting against his opponents. By the fourth/tenth century, as mentioned already, all non-Shi'i Muslims (except for the groups known as Kharijites) had come to recognize 'Ali as one of four rightly guided caliphs. Most deemed Mu'awiya to have been in error (some even said he was guilty of unbelief) when he fought against 'Ali at Siffin. As regards the battle of the Camel, the Sunnis now said that both 'Ali and his opponents had been right in their actions. They justified this by suggesting that the warring factions had all reached their decisions on the basis of *ijtihad* or individual reasoning (an admissible method in the Sunni schools of law and in Mu'tazilism, but still inadmissible in Imamism in the time of Mufid). The Mu'tazila, whose doctrine was becoming increasingly pro-'Alid, also condemned Mu'awiya as a sinner (some said he was an unbeliever) but, in the interest of harmony among Muslims, they were reluctant to condemn 'Ali's opponents at the battle of the Camel. Thus, they came up with the idea that the latter had repented of their rebellion against 'Ali before their death.

These positions, though favorable towards 'Ali, were still unacceptable to Imamis. For them 'Ali had been endowed with infallibility in all his acts and sayings. Furthermore, he had never practised *ijtihad*, which they regarded as a faulty method that engenders doubt and does not lead to certainty of religious knowledge. It followed that his opponents had been always and unequivocally in the wrong. According to Mufid, being

companions (of the Prophet) did not in itself preclude the possibility of error, forgetfulness, inadvertence, or even deliberate
disobedience of God's commands on their part.

Mufid endeavoured to prove from the mainstream historical
accounts that 'Ali always acted justly and that by acting against
him his opponents committed grave errors. He wrote a large
work in vindication of 'Ali's role in those events and especially
in the battle of the Camel. Against the Mu'tazili position which
sought to rehabilitate 'A'isha and her partners as true believers,
Mufid cited numerous reports showing that 'A'isha continued
to express enmity and ill-feeling towards 'Ali and even rejoiced
at the news of his death.

In addition to discussing and commenting on the events of
'Ali's caliphate as they appeared in the mainstream accounts,
Mufid included in his works a considerable number of speeches
by (or ascribed to) 'Ali. 'Ali was widely recognized as a great
orator, even beyond Shi'ism, and the texts of a number of his
speeches (or speeches ascribed to him) are found in Sunni
sources. Most of those included by Mufid, however, do not
appear in those sources; they serve specifically Imami concerns
and polemical needs. In some of them 'Ali comments on the
events of his own caliphate as they occur, and so we get to know
what he himself is supposed to have thought of those events and
why he acted in the way he did in various circumstances. As may
be expected, what 'Ali says in those speeches supports the
Imami interpretation of the *Fitna* and other episodes in early
Islamic history. With regards to the issue of whether or not 'Ali
himself had recognized the first three caliphs, Mufid cites several speeches which indicate that he did not. These show 'Ali
criticizing the caliphs for occupying a position that was right-
fully his and, as such, undermine the objection of opponents
that 'Ali was not known to have contested the accession of the
first three caliphs and even gave them the oath of allegiance.

THE OTHER IMAMS

Although much of Mufid's efforts were clearly directed towards proving that 'Ali was an Imami imam, he did not neglect the imamates of 'Ali's successors. As in his treatment of 'Ali's imamate, he concentrated on those aspects of their imamates that were the subject of criticism by opponents, both Shi'i and other. And here too, he selected some of his material from the mainstream chroniclers and other Shi'i sources.

The Imams' Relations with the Ruling Authorities

Opponents of Imamis would often object that the known facts about the lives and actions of their imams did not permit the conclusion that they had regarded themselves as Imami imams. For example, according to the mainstream historical tradition, 'Ali's son Hasan, the second imam of the Imamis, claimed the caliphate after 'Ali's death but soon afterwards abdicated in favour of Mu'awiya. He accepted a sum of money in return, made a peace agreement with him, and lived the rest of his life in comfort in Medina. From the point of view of opponents these were not the actions of someone who considered himself to be an Imami imam.

The accounts given by Mufid serve as a corrective: Hasan's decision to make peace with Mu'awiya had been motivated by his desire to prevent bloodshed among Muslims. Moreover, contrary to what some accounts maintain, Hasan did not die a natural death. Mu'awiya had him poisoned. (This claim is also found in some of the Sunni accounts.) This version of events made it possible for Mufid to argue that Hasan's actions did not amount to a renunciation of his own imamate, and that he would have certainly claimed it after Mu'awiya's death had he not been poisoned beforehand at the orders of this caliph. .

Another controversial episode in the history of the imams concerned the eighth Imami imam, 'Ali al-Rida, and his designation by the 'Abbasid caliph Ma'mun as his successor to the caliphate. In the event Ma'mun's plans came to nothing as 'Ali al-Rida later died in suspicious circumstances and, in the face of much opposition from the 'Abbasid family, the caliph abandoned his plans to transfer the caliphate to the 'Alids. From the point of view of opponents intent on undermining the Imami position, the arrangements made by Ma'mun must have entailed acquiescence on the part of 'Ali al-Rida who, after all, had married one of the caliph's daughters. The historical accounts were suggestive of his acquiescence or, at least, there was nothing in them which might indicate otherwise. Opponents could therefore argue that 'Ali al-Rida's willingness to go along with Ma'mun's plans and to accede to the caliphate as his successor was incompatible with the claims of his followers concerning his status as an imam. For Imamis, however, 'Ali al-Rida had been an unwilling instrument of Ma'mun's designs and had actually been poisoned at the orders of the caliph. The account given by Mufid serves to make this amply clear.

Rival Claimants to the Imamate

A historical defense of the imamate involved refuting the claims of other 'Alids or claims on their behalf, which had been made during the lives of Imami imams. By the time of Mufid, and even earlier, some of the movements that had arisen in favor of other 'Alids had long ceased to have any adherents. They were of little or no interest to Mufid. Of more immediate relevance were those early movements which the contemporary Zaydis and the Isma'ilis recognized as their predecessors. Mufid appears to have been far more interested in refuting the Zaydi doctrine of the imamate than he was the Isma'ili. This may be related to the fact that in the Buyid period Zaydi and Imami scholars competed for recognition and acceptance of their respective versions of Shi'ism, especially among the ruling élite who were in a position to give appointments and provide patronage. (For a suggestion concerning the apparent lack of interest of Buyid scholars in refuting Isma'ilism, see above, Chapter 2.)

There was another aspect to this rivalry, involving the Mu'tazilis with whom the Imamis were also polemically engaged. Leading scholars of the Mu'tazila had come to recognize some of the past imams of the Zaydis as having had the right qualifications for, and hence a legitimate claim to, the imamate. Those imams included Zayd b. 'Ali, who was the half-brother of the fifth Imami imam, Muhammad al-Baqir, and after whom the Zaydis were named; and the Hasanid 'Alid Muhammad b. 'Abdallah (known in the tradition as the Pure Soul). This recognition of Zaydi imams by the Mu'tazila would have made it even more important that Mufid attempt to show that those imams did not have a legitimate claim.

In the case of Zayd b. 'Ali, Mufid attempted to refute the claim concerning his imamate by recasting him as a believer in the Imami imamate. Zayd had rebelled against the Umayyads in 122/739 in the hope of securing the caliphate. This was during the time of his nephew Ja'far al-Sadiq, who is believed to have occupied the position of sixth Imami imam. According to Mufid, Zayd's rebellion was undertaken in order to secure the imamate not for himself but for Ja'far. Such a view of Zayd's intentions has no support in any of the earlier sources that report or discuss those events. Mufid mentions it nonetheless as it serves to undermine Zaydism by showing its key figure as having been a supporter of the Imami imamate.

It was also during the time of Ja'far al-Sadiq that another 'Alid, the Hasanid Muhammad the Pure Soul, together with his brother Ibrahim, led an uprising against the 'Abbasids in Medina and Iraq and were killed in the ensuing hostilities in 145/762. Muhammad was believed by many to have been the awaited 'Alid Mahdi during his life, and after his death some of his followers continued to expect that he would return in order to fulfil this role. He was still revered by many inside and outside Shi'ism in the fourth/tenth century. According to the Imami tradition, Ja'far al-Sadiq had rejected Muhammad's claims and even predicted the failure of his uprising and his killing at the hands of the 'Abbasids. Ja'far's predictions were taken to be evidence of the error of Zaydi activism and of the view that the quietism advocated by the Imami imams was divinely inspired. Mufid cites a set of reports which convey the same point. He tells us that his reports have been extracted from the book of Abu al-Faraj Isfahani, a Zaydi author who was his near-contemporary. Clearly though, and as elsewhere in his works, when he quotes non-Imami reports as additional proof of authenticity, these reports have been subjected to Imami interpretations and supplemented with Imami material.

In the account of Mufid the reports concerning Ja'far's negative attitude to the uprising of Muhammad the Pure Soul become an occasion for proving that the Imami doctrine of the twelfth imam as the Mahdi had been established long before the twelfth imam went into occultation. According to the Imami tradition, the names and identities of the twelve imams had been revealed to the Prophet and this information was preserved in a book which passed to his daughter Fatima and from her to the imams among her descendants. In Mufid's account Ja'far is shown to have rejected the belief that Muhammad the Pure Soul was the Mahdi because, as he told Muhammad's father, the time of the Mahdi had not yet arrived; the implication is that Ja'far already knew who the true Mahdi was going to be.

There is another indication of the importance of
Zaydi–Imami polemic as a factor in Mufid's accounts of the
lives of the imams. This concerns the doctrine of "the most
excellent." Both the Imamis and the Zaydis maintained that
only the most excellent of the community could be the rightful
imam. For both sects excellence was conceived in terms of
knowledge of religious matters, though other qualifications
such as piety and justice were also important. Thus, where an
'Alid recognized by Zaydis as one of their imams was known to
have been active during the time of an Imami imam, and had
challenged (or perhaps, appeared in retrospect to have to challenged) the claim of that imam, one of the questions for the dis-
puting sects was who of the two 'Alids had been "the most
excellent."

In his account of the career and martyrdom of Muhammad
the Pure Soul, the Zaydi author Abu al-Faraj Isfahani speaks of
him as the best of the Family of the Prophet and the greatest
man of his time in religious learning and courage. Mufid does
not refer to this part of Isfahani's account. However, his own
account of the imamate of Ja'far al-Sadiq appears to contain an
indirect response to Isfahani's claims in favor of Muhammad
the Pure Soul. Thus, Mufid tells us that in virtue and in learning
Ja'far was the most distinguished of his brothers and other
members of the Family of the Prophet. The amount of traditional knowledge transmitted from him far exceeds anything
transmitted from other members. Miracles and divine signs
appeared "by his hands" (or through his intermediacy) and he
was given knowledge of things unseen. By the fourth/tenth
century miracles by the imam had come to be regarded as one
of two means by which his imamate is established, the other
being personal designation by his predecessor.

For the rest, Mufid's discussion of the lives of the imams consists of elaborations on themes and problems familiar from the

works of earlier Imami scholars. The imams are shown to have possessed the weapons of the Prophet, yet another proof that they (and not the descendants of Hasan, viz. the Zaydi imams) inherited his authority. They were distinguished by their superior knowledge, especially in religious matters. The ninth imam, who was believed to have acceded to the imamate as a minor, was able to demonstrate that he had perfect knowledge of the law and, therefore, that minority does not invalidate the imamate of a true imam.

The Twelfth Imam / the Mahdi

According to classical Imami doctrine, the twelfth imam was born in 255/869. His birth was kept secret because of fear for his life, and it was known only to a few close and trusted associates of his father. When his father died in 260/874 he went into a state of occultation, communicating with his followers through a series of four deputies. All communication then came to an end in 329/941 when he entered into a state of "greater occultation." This occultation is also an earthly state of existence, but during it no one could claim to represent him. It will last until the end of time. His appearance and rising as the Mahdi will be sometime before the Day of Judgment, when he will rule the world and justice will prevail. He will restore Islam to its original perfection and enforce the law as taught by the imams.

Unlike the other eleven imams about whom some historical information exists outside Imamism, the twelfth imam was never seen by outsiders and his very existence was questioned by opponents and, for a time, by many Imamis. Doubts concerning his existence increased with time and as the period of his absence began to exceed a normal lifespan. An Imami scholar by the name of Nu'mani, who wrote the oldest extant work on the subject in 342/953, complained that most Imamis did not know who the hidden imam was and some even disputed his existence. Similar remarks were made by Ibn Babuya (d. 381/991) in a well-known treatise entitled "The Perfection of Religion and the Completion of Grace in Confirming the Occultation and Removing Confusion." In this work the Imami doctrine of the occultation more or less achieved its classical form. Nevertheless, throughout the fifth/eleventh century Imami scholars, including Mufid, continued to write on the subject and to defend the occultation in the face of attacks by outsiders.

Ibn Babuya had sought to demonstrate the existence of the twelfth imam in a state of occultation almost entirely by arguments from the Qur'an and traditional sources, and he attempted to justify the prolongation of the occultation by adducing traditional material about biblical and other figures who were believed to have lived very long lives. Mufid, on the other hand, although he did not ignore arguments from tradition, was convinced of the value of a reasoned defense of this doctrine. He wrote a number of theological treatises on the subject, which will be discussed in the next chapter.

In his account of the life of the twelfth imam, Mufid was aware of the problem that absolutely nothing had been reported about him outside Imamism. But he was not too bothered about this because, according to him, the rational proofs for the existence of the twelfth imam are sufficient and render superfluous the evidence of proof texts and reports. His account consisted of Hadith reports concerning the twelfth imam's designation, predictions by the Prophet and the other imams about his occultation, and reports showing that he was seen by a number of reliable Imamis and that he maintained contact with his community during the time of his "lesser occultation."

At the end of his account, and as if to reinforce the point that the rising of the Mahdi will be at the end of times, Mufid gave a very long list of the signs that will precede the event. The nature and number of those signs are such that no one could claim that the time has arrived for this to occur. They include the appearance of impostors in Syria and Yemen, a voice from heaven calling the name of the Mahdi, the swallowing up in the desert of an army sent by the Syrian impostor, the rising of the sun in the west, and a lunar eclipse in the middle of the month of Ramadan.

4

THE IMAMATE: THE
RATIONAL ARGUMENTS

We have seen that Mufid devoted much time and space to
the sacred history of the imamate and its defense on the
basis of arguments derived from the historical sources. But he
was also thoroughly acquainted with the theological discourse
of his time and realized that Hadith and other traditional
sources, which other Imami scholars tended to rely on extensively and with the minimum of reasoning, were not sufficient.
As the polemic against Imamis widened and their traditions
and writings came under closer scrutiny, there was a need for
new solutions and new approaches. Moreover, Imamism had to
be defended against the charge of rationalist theologians
that many of its doctrines were not compatible with reason. As
will be discussed more fully in the next chapter, Mufid admitted reason as one of the valid sources of religious knowledge,
albeit one that is dependent on revelation, and he was clearly
in favor of engaging in *kalam* theology and defended this
against the objections of Imami traditionalists. With regards to
the Imami imamate, Mufid's detailed rational arguments in
its defense became the framework for all later works on the
subject.

In Mufid's day, discussions about the imamate were to a
large extent centered on the occultation of the twelfth

imam. Mu'tazili and other theologians continued to attack Imamis for what they saw as an intrinsic contradiction in their doctrine: the necessity of the imamate, and the fact that the imam of the time was in a state of occultation; or, how an imam whose role as religious guide was deemed to be necessary can ever be said to be absent. Mufid wrote several treatises devoted to justification of the occultation and sought to demonstrate rationally that it is perfectly compatible with the doctrine of necessity of the imamate. He also dealt with questions concerning the nature and qualities of the imams, which were still being debated within Imamism and disputed with outsiders.

In all his theological expositions of the doctrine of the imamate the idea of the imam as sole authoritative teacher of religion after the Prophet remained axiomatic. The idea distinguished Imamism from Sunni and Mu'tazili Islam, where the imam or caliph was regarded as essentially a political leader with no authority to dispense religious instruction.

THE NECESSITY OF THE IMAMATE

One of the earliest attested Imami arguments in support of the necessity of the imamate was that it guards religion against divergence in beliefs and practices. This argument was used against the evolving Sunni position which admitted legal divergence as divinely sanctioned. With the end of the line of visible imams, and as Imamis came to collect and codify their Hadith reports, they too had to deal with the problem of divergence. As before, they continued to insist that divergence did not actually exist in the teachings of the imams and that it was due to imperfect transmission of those teachings by disciples. Still, the persistence of the problem meant that the idea of doctrinal uniformity as a main argument for the necessity of the imamate lost much of its force; if it was mentioned again it was usually in passing.

But the Imami imam was (or, rather, by the late third/ninth century, had come to be) more than an infallible guide to Islamic law and doctrine. He was the link between God and mankind or, as Imamis put it, he was God's Proof on earth. Thus, when Imamis accepted that all contact between the imam and his community came to an end, this did not entail regarding the institution as redundant. On the contrary, they continued to uphold and defend its necessity and the duty to acknowledge the (now hidden) imam of the time. In fact, the particular formulation of the Imami doctrine of the twelfth imam as the Mahdi was to a large extent determined by the emphasis that early Imamis had placed on the permanent need for a rightful imam: the Mahdi may be in occultation but he continues to exist on earth.

Before Mufid Imami scholars tended to argue for the necessity of the imamate almost entirely from the Qur'an and the traditions of the Prophet and the imams. According to one of the most commonly cited Imami Hadith reports, "The earth can never be devoid of Proof. If it should ever become devoid of Proof it would disappear and swallow up all who are on it." According to a reported statement by the Prophet, "Whoever dies without having acknowledged his imam dies the death of one from the Age of Ignorance." (This statement was recognized as authentic by other Muslims, but tended to be interpreted differently, for example, in the sense that one had to recognize a rightly guided imam whenever one existed. The Age of Ignorance referred to the pre-Islamic period when Arabs or people in general were "ignorant of God.") A Qur'anic verse (Q. 4: 59) in which believers are urged to obey God, the Prophet, and "those in authority among you" was interpreted by Imamis as another proof of the necessity of the imamate.

To this Mufid added an argument "from reason and reflection." People, he said, are legally dependent on the imams in that they have been ordered to obey them, to refer their disputes to them, and to seek knowledge from them. The imams are also needed for executing the law and for establishing obligations such as the pilgrimage, holy war, and almsgiving. It follows that people are required to have definite knowledge of them, otherwise God would be obliging people to do what they cannot fulfill. In other words, since God is just he would establish the identity of the imams beyond any doubt so that people can know and fulfill the duties that He imposes upon them.

We have here one of the instances where Mufid has used a Mu'tazili principle in order to strengthen Imami doctrine, namely, that God's justice necessitates that He provide guidance to mankind. In Mu'tazilism this "guidance" is envisaged in terms of human reason and the revelation of God's will to prophets. Mufid, however, extended the principle to cover the guidance of the imams.

THE IMAMS' INFALLIBILITY

In early Imamism the idea of the imams' infallibility had been conceived as relevant mainly to their knowledge and teaching of the law. They were regarded as custodians of the revelation to the Prophet Muhammad in the sense of perfect transmitters of that revelation, and not in the sense of independent makers of or contributors to the law. By the late third/ninth century, however, the imams had come to be regarded as infallible in all their acts, as well as in their knowledge. This was part of the process whereby the status of the imamate was enhanced and its nature transformed under the influence of gnostic and messianic currents, and as a result of which it became no longer possible, or even necessary, to distinguish between two concepts of infallibility (that of knowledge and that of acts) or to uphold one and reject the other.

Initially, in the second/eighth century, Imamis did not accord infallibility to the Prophet Muhammad or to any other prophet. (Their reasoning then was that prophets, unlike imams, receive revelations and could be corrected if they erred in their judgments, hence they do not have to be endowed with infallibility.) However, when other Muslims began to affirm the infallibility of the Prophet, the Imami position changed, and by the middle of the third/ninth century Imamis had come to regard all prophets as infallible. Another development, attested in the thought of Ibn Babuya, was that the imams and prophets, though immune from major and minor sins, are liable to commit errors inadvertently. It was said that God might cause them to commit such errors in order to prove to their followers that they are human.

Mufid upheld the infallibility of the imams' acts and knowledge, as well as the infallibility of all prophets. He argued that since the imam takes the place of a prophet as religious guide, he must, like him, be protected from error and sin. In his view, an imam's infallibility and perfect religious knowledge, as well as the fallibility and imperfect knowledge of those who claimed the imamate during his own time, is proof of the validity of his own imamate.

Regarding the possibility of errors committed inadvertently, Mufid rejected the view of his teacher Ibn Babuya. He accepted, however, that it is possible for an imam to commit minor sins before he acceeds to his position. In his view this is also possible for other prophets except Muhammad.

Given these views, one would expect Mufid to have come to the conclusion that in the matter of personal excellence the imams are equal to prophets. But he does not, probably because he realizes, as he himself admits, that the weight of the evidence from the Imami tradition supports the superiority of the imams over all previous prophets except Muhammad. So he prefers to leave the question open. He says this is a question over which Imamis are not agreed and which reason cannot determine one way or the other.

THE IMAMS' KNOWLEDGE

Contemporary Imami literature was full of traditional material testifying to the divine sources and virtually unlimited scope of the imams' knowledge. These reports and the beliefs expressed in them were not always universally accepted within Imamism. Earlier generations of Imami scholars who lived during the time of the imams would have regarded many of them as heretical "exaggeration." We know of a number of scholars who held the view that the imams' knowledge was based entirely on transmission from the Prophet and who rejected the idea of the imams as recipients of divinely imparted knowledge. According to those early scholars, the imams were indeed endowed with infallibility, but this was conceived as an ability to understand, preserve, and transmit the knowledge they received from the Prophet and not as something engendered by receipt of knowledge directly from the divine realm.

This early moderate view of the imams' knowledge had been specifically formulated to be compatible with the doctrine of Muhammad as "the seal of prophets," which was widely held among Muslim scholars and signified acceptance of the notion that all communication between God and mankind had come to an end with his death. Eventually, and as Imamism began to absorb much of the speculations of Shi'i messianists and gnostics, that view was almost completely overshadowed and the imams came be regarded as prophets in all but name. Imamis continued to uphold the doctrine of Muhammad as "the seal of prophets," but they had to reformulate their doctrine of the imams' knowledge in such a way as to make it compatible with the former. Their solution was to use different terms to describe the divine communications to prophets and to imams and to distinguish between the manners in which knowledge was passed to them. Thus, the imams were said to receive divine inspiration (*ilham*), not revelation (*wahy*) which is the prerogative of prophets. And whereas prophets had the ability to see the angelic creatures who were the agents of revelation (for example, the angel Gabriel, in the case of the Prophet), the imams could only hear their voices. The "Spoken to" (*muhaddath*) became one of the epithets of the Imami imams.

The adoption by Imamism of the doctrine of inspiration raised another set of theoretical problems which were frequently picked up by opponents. Thus, for example, opponents objected that inspiration implies that the imams had access to knowledge of religious matters which had not been available to the Prophet. Imami traditionalists had attempted to resolve this by citing reports suggesting that whenever information was imparted to an imam by means of inspiration it was simultaneously made known to the Prophet and all the other imams in their posthumous state of existence. Mufid, on the other hand, whilst by no means denying the possibility of inspiration, seems to have adhered to the view (attested in early Imamism and also upheld by his pupil Tusi) that the imams' knowledge of the law was derived entirely from the Prophet and acquired by each imam by transmission from his predecessor. This may be inferred from, among other things, his insistence that the imams knew the answer to any legal problem which arose and did not have to wait for inspiration or to rely on personal opinion.

The traditionalists also accepted without questioning the reports which attributed to the imams the ability to read the thoughts of men, to tell the future, and to speak in all languages. Mufid, on the other hand, sought to restrict the scope and nature of the imams' knowledge by subjecting the reports to rational analysis. He argued that reason does not necessitate that the imams have the ability to know the future, to read the minds of others, or to hear the voices of angels. It is just possible that God occasionally granted them this ability as a favor and in order that their followers should believe in their imamate and obey them.

The position taken by Mufid on the question of inspiration, that it is possible but not necessary, enabled him to deal with difficult questions such as one posed to him regarding 'Ali's murder. He was asked why 'Ali decided to go into the mosque at Kufa if he knew that his killer would be waiting for him there. Mufid replied that there is no consensus among the Imamiyya that the imams had access to knowledge of the future. Moreover, reason only necessitates that they know the legal status of everything that happens.

A somewhat different view of the imams' knowledge of the future was expressed by Mufid when he was asked how, given that the imams do not receive revelations, the hidden imam would know whether the time was right for his uprising, whether a sufficient number of loyal and determined warriors were available to support his uprising, and whether it would be successful? Here, Mufid replied that the imams have been covenanted to undertake certain actions and (for this reason) they have been given knowledge of things to come and signs indicating to them what actions to take and what the consequences of their actions will be. They have this knowledge by transmission from the Prophet through whom the covenant was made and who received it by revelation.

THE IMAMS AND THE QUR'AN

In early Islam there arose a debate about whether the official text of the Qur'an, which had been collected by the third caliph 'Uthman, contained all the revelations that the Prophet received and recited in the presence of his disciples over a period of twenty years. The idea of the Qur'an's "incompleteness" is found, for example, in reports about verses and passages that have gone missing, and some of which people still remembered and transmitted. We also hear of other complete or partial collections of the Qur'an, which had been made by other companions of the Prophet and which contained words and phrases that diverged from the official text; none of those collections, it must be added, is extant. Those credited with "non-official" collections include 'Ali and the first two caliphs, Abu Bakr and 'Umar.

According to modern research, the debate about the completeness or otherwise of the Qur'an and the existence of variant readings arose within the context of second/eighth century attempts by Muslim jurists to elaborate the law and to define its sources. Some were inclined to regard the Qur'an as the only admissible source and rejected the authority of oral tradition and personal opinion. Under the pressure of such views, there arose the idea that some rules and practices which have no basis in the text of the Qur'an are based on missing verses. And rules which were perceived to be at odds with the Qur'an were said to have been based on variant codices. These scripturalist views failed, however, to gain acceptance among most jurists. This is because the Qur'an does not contain much legal material and, as the elaboration of Muslim law proceeded, most scholars came to accept the Sunna of the Prophet, as preserved in the oral tradition, the Hadith, as another revealed source. Moreover, the idea of missing revelations was eventually denied by most Muslims, as it laid them open to attack by Jews and Christians whom they themselves would often accuse of having falsified and altered their respective scriptures.

In Imamism the idea that some revelations were missing from the official text seems to have survived longer. Two factors are likely to have contributed to this. Firstly, the idea could be used against the Sunni caliphate and in favour of 'Ali and the Imami imamate. 'Uthman could be accused of having failed to collect the complete Qur'an, and 'Ali could be said to have composed the only complete and authentic version. In making those claims the Imamis were able to draw on reports circulating among Sunnis, which credited 'Ali with the first collection. They maintained that in fact 'Ali had been entrusted with this task by the Prophet and that 'Uthman and other enemies of 'Ali had deliberately avoided consulting the latter's version of the Qur'an or making it the basis of the official recension. 'Ali's copy was said to have passed down to the imams.

Secondly, the idea of additional revelations was of some value to an early Imami view of the relation between the imams and the Qur'an. Not only were the imams regarded as the sole authoritative interpreters of the Qur'an; their teachings were said to have been based entirely on it. Thus, the idea that the imams had a complete version could serve to support the claim concerning the Qur'anic basis of all their teachings. If outsiders objected that for certain teachings no link could be established with the Qur'an that is known to everyone, Imamis could argue that this was because those teachings were based on the additional revelations known only to the imams.

This scripturalist position was eventually abandoned by Imamis, and the doctrine of additional Qur'anic revelations was toned down and modified. Like other Muslims, Imamis came to accept the idea of Prophetic practice (or Sunna as expressed in Hadith) as a second revealed source in addition to the Qur'an. They also came to adopt a view concerning the 'Alid codex, which was more moderate than the idea that it contained additional revelations. It was now presented as one of the variant codices whose existence was recognized in the Sunni tradition. It was said to have differed from the official text only in the order of its chapters and in that it contained a few additional or different words, mostly references to 'Ali and the imamate. It was also said to have contained exegetical comments or interpretations written by 'Ali in its margin, in other words, the additional material was not Qur'anic. It was taken into hiding by the twelfth imam and its exact contents and structure will become fully known only upon his appearance. The imams were said to have instructed the believers to continue to recite the Qur'an according to the official version until the appearance of the Mahdi.

A further step in the direction of accommodating the Imami view of the Qur'an to the prevalent Sunni position was taken by Ibn Babuya. He affirmed that the text which is "between the two covers," that is to say, the received text, is complete and unaltered.

Mufid's extant works show that his position on the question of additional revelations in 'Ali's text (and omissions from the official text) changed. As he himself indicates, at first he defended the view that 'Ali had made a complete and perfect collection and that the additional revelations were now in the hands of the hidden imam.

He dealt with one of the most common objections against the existence of an 'Alid Qur'an, namely, that if 'Ali had really compiled one then why was it not published? Imamis tended to deal with this criticism on the basis that 'Ali did not wish to antagonize 'Uthman and the other caliphs or to expose Muslims to open conflict. But this explanation was rejected by opponents. They could point to reports about two other companions of the Prophet who published their variant codices with no adverse consequences. Against that Mufid argued that the two cases were different. 'Ali was a far more influential figure and an opponent, whereas the two companions were among the followers of the caliphs and, hence, there was not much harm to people from the publication of their texts. He makes no mention of another common objection which said that if 'Uthman had really falsified the text, 'Ali should have been able to put things right when he became caliph.

On the question of what attitude the believers should take towards the official text, Mufid cited instructions by the imams that until the rise of the Mahdi they should follow this text in their recitations. The imams, he added, forbade us to recite the additional and variant words that occur in some traditions because the latter are single-authority reports and, hence, subject to error in transmission.

Thus, the first position taken by Mufid was that there have been omissions from the 'Uthmanic Qur'an, that the 'Alid Qur'an contained all the revelations made to the Prophet and was now in the hands of the Mahdi, but that nothing of its contents can be known from the existing traditions. Later, however, he modified his position and stated that he was in favor of the thesis that "no word, verse, or chapter" is missing from the official text, although, as he says, he has found no conclusive rational argument against the view which asserted that omissions were made. He was able to justify this (later) position by suggesting that the Imami Hadith reports about the completeness of the 'Alid Qur'an referred to the interpretation or exegetical comments in the margin, and not to the text itself.

THE IMAMS' MIRACLES

In the time of Mufid much of the theological polemic of the Mu'tazila was directed at Imamis and other groups whose views concerning the possibility of miracles seemed to undermine the special status of the Prophet within Islam. The Sufis, as Muslim mystics were known, believed that the "elect" had the ability not only to communicate with the divine but also to perform miracles. In Isma'ili and Imami Shi'ism similar claims were made for the imams. Against such claims, Mu'tazili scholars sought to demonstrate that miracles are exclusively a sign of the prophetic office.

Mufid insisted that miracles were one of the proofs of an imam's claim to the imamate, the other main proof being an explicit statement of designation by his predecessor. As he tells us, numerous Hadith reports existed about the miracles the imams performed and the "signs" they received during their lives. He accepts those traditions as well-attested and valid, although, as he admits, he is not able to support them with rational proofs. As in the case of his argument regarding the ability of the imams to receive divine communication, he says reason does not necessitate that they work miracles, neither does it preclude it.

His response to Mu'tazili objections was to prove them invalid by showing that miracles by the imams are *not* impossible on the basis of reason. An example of this may be found in his comments on an account he gives of a miraculous incident involving 'Ali. According to this account, during one of his campaigns in Arabia the Prophet dispatched 'Ali at the head of a small contingent in order to confront a horde of *jinn* (invisible beings) who did not believe in Muhammad's prophethood and were intent on harming his followers. 'Ali succeeded in fighting off most of them and the rest submitted to the Prophet and believed in him. Mufid tells us that the report has been transmitted by Sunnis as well as by Shi'is. This, he says, is one indication of its authenticity. (We may recall here the Mu'tazili argument that Hadith reports about the Imami imamate, even when transmitted from multiple witnesses, do not constitute valid proof because they have been transmitted within Imamism only.) He attacks the Mu'tazila for claiming that the report is contrary to reason. He says the Qur'an, which itself is of a miraculous nature, speaks of *jinn* and refers to their belief in Muhammad and the revelation to him (Q. 72: 1–2). This establishes beyond any doubt the existence of *jinn*. It also renders invalid the Mu'tazila's rejection on rational grounds of the reports of 'Ali's encounter with *jinn*.

THE IMAMS AFTER DEATH

One of the puzzling positions taken by Mufid concerns the state of the imams after death. He taught that whilst in this life, the imams and prophets are physically exactly the same as other men. After death, however, they are transported in body and soul from their graves to the Garden of God where they remain living in bliss and rejoicing in the righteous believers who join them. Whilst there they are kept informed by God of the condition and acts of the faithful in this world, and they hear the words addressed to them by the faithful at their shrines.

Some aspects of this teaching have echoes in the early Imami Hadith tradition. There the imams and prophets are referred to as in some kind of posthumous existence where they continue to receive knowledge about the acts of men – a belief that was probably related to their role as intercessors. However, the idea that their bodies do not remain in their graves is not clearly attested in the early Imami tradition or for any scholar before Mufid. Mufid tells us that it is the common belief among Imami Hadith scholars and jurists. But it may well have been a relatively recent development. There is some suggestion from Mufid's own treatment of the subject that, according to a current popular belief, the imams were alive *in their graves* and could hear from there the invocations of their followers.

In any case, Mufid preferred the belief which said that the imams were, soul and body, in the Garden. He clearly did not think it rationally possible that anyone remains alive in the grave, and he could present his own position as defensible on the basis of both reason and revelation. It was after all common belief among Muslims that the eventual fate of all believers would be resurrection and eternal life in Paradise.

That is not to say, of course, that Mufid was opposed to the manifestations of popular piety which took place at the imams' shrines. On the contrary, as we shall see in the last chapter, he recognized the importance of those shrines and the pilgrimages to them in the process of consolidation of the Imami community. This is clearly reflected in the work he wrote on pilgrimages to the shrines, where he described in detail the rituals to be performed, the procedures to be followed, what to say when addressing the imams and invoking their intercession, and so forth. He also defended strongly the idea of rituals performed at empty graves as a valid and meaningful act of worship. One of the arguments he used was based on analogy with the rituals performed at the Ka'ba in Mecca. God, he says, has imposed on mankind the duty of visiting and circumambulating His House (the Ka'ba) even though no place encloses Him and He is not nearer to any one place than to another. Similarly,

God has ordained that the tombs of the imams be visited as shrines even though their bodies are not in them.

UNACCEPTABLE EXAGGERATION

As discussed briefly in the Introduction, the dominant trend in early Imamism was legalist and opposed to all the messianic and gnostic manifestations that arose within Shiʻism. Leading Imamis saw it as their task to protect Imamism from those other currents and to prevent the incursion of their ideas and beliefs among the ranks of the faithful. In fact, the first work on Muslim sects (or "sects and heretical doctrines," as the genre came to be known among Muslims) was composed by an Imami scholar whose main aim was to refute the non-Imami and extremist Shiʻi groups. A related genre of writing, known as "the refutation of exaggeration," also appeared among Imamis. Sunni and Muʻtazili scholars drew heavily on this material when they came to compose their own works on Muslim sects.

The term and the concept used in those works to describe doctrinal extremism in Shiʻism was *ghuluww* (lit., exaggeration). In its narrow sense the term referred to elevating the status of one's imam to the level of prophet, redeemer, or divine incarnation. But it was also applied to a whole series of related beliefs. Thus, for example, the belief of messianic Shiʻis that their imam received divine messages of an apocalyptic nature was characterized by early Imamis as exaggeration because it implied that an imam was a prophet. The belief that an imam went into a state of occultation and the expectation that he would return as the redeemer were also deemed to be exaggeration. Similarly, in addition to the deification of their imam, the Shiʻi gnostics were criticized by Imamis for harboring the following exaggerated beliefs: antinomianism, the transmigration of souls, and the existence of the "World of Shadows" — the spiritual sphere or "sphere of light" of gnostic myths of the creation.

As mentioned previously, the fight against exaggeration led by Imami legalists in the third/ninth century was not entirely successful. By the time of the occultation, Imamism had come to incorporate numerous beliefs and ideas which it had previously labeled as exaggeration. This was not a process of *fusion* of legalist and gnostic conceptions of the imamate, or a wholesale acceptance of gnostic doctrine by the legalists. The process, rather, consisted of adapting and incorporating *elements* from those other currents and rejecting others. The gnostic elements admitted are still recognizable but they have lost their original significance when integrated into the essentially legalist Imami structure. Some elements have been toned down and modified so as to be more compatible with generally recognized Islamic principles, namely, the absolute unity of God, the cessation of prophecy with the death of Muhammad, and the paramount authority of the law. Other elements, which were thought to undermine one or more of these principles, tended not to find their way into the classical collections of Imami Hadith, and they continued to be refuted by Imami and other heresiographers as exaggeration.

Thus, for example, under the influence of the gnostic currents the Imami imams came to be credited with many of the attributes of spiritual saviors. They were said to have been endowed with limitless knowledge, including that of the unseen. They had the ability to perform miracles. They had miraculous births. They remained alive after death. They were in the same rank as prophets. They were created out of divine light before the creation of the world. Yet, they were neither prophets nor divine incarnations, and they had no inherent

knowledge of divine mysteries. They do not appear in the role
of initiating in man a process of spiritual salvation or of acquiring esoteric knowledge. Though belief in them was essential for
salvation, it was not sufficient. Imamis continued to uphold the
traditional view of salvation and to denounce as exaggeration
the antinomianism of the gnosticizers, their tendency to refute
the resurrection and reward and punishment in heaven and
hell, the doctrine of transmigration of souls, and the deification
of the imams or the belief that they are divine incarnations.

By the early part of the fourth/tenth century, the pheno-
menon of exaggeration was no longer a major internal problem
for Imamism. The borderline between acceptable doctrine and
exaggeration had been more or less drawn, and the gnostic currents had found more hospitable terrain in Isma'ili and Nusayri
Shi'ism. Moreover, the Imami leadership in Baghdad had the
backing of the state in its attempt to impose a relatively moderate doctrine of the imamate. This was demonstrated on two
occasions (in 309/922 and 322/934) when, at the instigation
of Imami leaders, two men, the famous mystic Hallaj, and
Shalmaghani (whose claim to represent the hidden imam was
opposed by the Imami leadership who supported their own
candidate), were arrested and prosecuted for advocating
extremist beliefs, and were subsequently executed.

But although the gnostic elements had been neutralized and
had long ceased to be a threat to the legalist character of
Imamism, with the development of theological debate, some of
those elements were found to be incompatible with other
ideas, for example, about the human soul. Of particular interest were Hadith reports, which can still be found in canonical
Imami collections, consisting of fragments of gnostic creation
myths. These speak of the souls (or shadows) of the imams (as
well as the souls/shadows of all prophets) as created out of
divine light in the World of Shadows. The World of Shadows is

said to have come into existence two thousand years before the creation of Adam and this world. The souls of all humans are said to have been created in it, the souls of Shiʿi believers out of a special substance.

Traditionalist Imami scholars, including Mufid's teacher Ibn Babuya, tended to accept these traditions at face value and saw them as evidence of the superior status of the imams and the fact that they and their followers belonged to the "saved party." They did not recognize the ideas expressed in them as a form of exaggeration, because these traditions envisaged the imams as "created" out of divine light, and this could appear to be quite distinct from the belief associated with exaggerators that the imams were "incarnations" of God or His light.

Mufid, however, refuted all these ideas as exaggeration. He was opposed to any belief which indicated that souls have a pre-existence, and from which one might conclude, as Ibn Babuya did, that they have a permanence independent of bodies. He accused Ibn Babuya of accepting isolated reports and of ignorance of their true meaning. He also accused him of holding a view of the soul similar to that held by philosophers and advocates of transmigration. It is views like these, he said, which laid Imamis open to the charge of dualism made against them by their Sunni opponents.

He suggested that the Hadith reports concerning the pre-existence of the imams and their creation in the "World of Shadows" consisted of embellishments and distortions by exaggerators who composed books on the subject and falsely ascribed their contents to truthful Imamis. He gave an alternative interpretation of the reports, which was more compatible with his own view of the soul and of the entirely human nature of the imams: the shadows of the imams that God created and were located on His throne were not living or reasoning souls but exact images of their human forms. When God created

Adam He made him see their images in order for him to glorify them and to know that they will be owed reverence and obedience and that the welfare of religion and this world will not be complete without them.

Mufid also reinterpreted the references to God's light so as to exclude any suggestion of "light" as a substance of incarnation and any notion that the souls of the imams were created from it. Thus, he tells us, when God created the images of the imams He placed light on them and intended this as a sign for Adam to realize that religion and the truth will be illuminated through them.

He dismissed the argument which said that the belief concerning the "creation" of the imams out of God's light did not entail deification and, therefore, was not exaggeration. He did this indirectly by discussing the doctrine known as delegationism, which was rejected by Imamis as a form of unmistakable exaggeration. Delegationism referred to the belief that the imams and the Prophet were lesser gods whom God created and to whom He "delegated" the creation of the world. Mufid explained that the delegationists differed from other exaggerators in their admission that the imams were not divine but created in time. Their belief in the createdness of the imams did not, however, change the fact that their doctrine of the imamate was reprehensible exaggeration. And although he does not say it in so many words, the same reasoning could be used to refute the "light" reports as transmitted and interpreted by traditionalists: the fact that they speak of the imams as "created" does not make them any more acceptable or devoid of exaggeration; other elements in them are still suggestive of a belief in divine incarnation.

Accusations of exaggeration were made against Mufid himself (and presumably against like-minded theologians) by traditionalist scholars. At one point Mufid defended his own doctrine of the imams' infallibility against the accusations of a traditionalist from the city of Qumm that it amounted to exaggeration. As mentioned above, Mufid denied the possibility that the prophets and the imams could commit small errors inadvertently. The Qummi scholar who, like Ibn Babuya, admitted such a possibility is reported by Mufid to have said that "the first degree in exaggeration is to deny the possibility of inadvertence on the part of prophets and imams." Mufid responded to this by accusing his Imami opponent of "falling short," that is, of underestimating the status of the imams.

These exchanges suggest that in the time of Mufid the concept of exaggeration was being used freely as a polemical tool in theological disputes between rationalists and traditionalists within Imamism, as well as against Imamism. Mufid used it in order to discredit beliefs about the nature of the imams which did not agree with his own doctrine of the soul, and his traditionalist opponents used it against him in order to discredit his view concerning the absolute infallibility of imams and prophets. There is nothing to indicate that its use reflected the existence of a gnostic doctrine among Imamis or, as has been suggested in a recent work, that Mufid and other rationalist theologians were responsible for the demise of a gnostic component within Imamism.

THE OCCULTATION OF THE TWELFTH IMAM

We have already said that in the fourth/tenth century the main problem for Imamism, and the focus of much of its scholarship, was the question of occultation of the twelfth imam. Imami treatises devoted to justification of the occultation and reconciling it with the belief in the necessity of the imamate were still being written well into the fifth/eleventh century. Earlier scholars who wrote on the subject were concerned mainly with demonstrating the existence of the twelfth imam in a state of occultation and they tended to rely on traditional sources. They would cite Hadith reports from the Prophet and the imams indicating that there will only be twelve imams and that one of the imams (or, more specifically, the twelfth imam) will go into occultation. The occultation was reconciled with the dictum that "the earth can never be devoid of an imam/divine Proof" on the basis that it is an earthly state of existence. The failure of the imam to appear as the Mahdi, even when conditions seemed favorable, was justified on the basis of Hadith reports indicating that God knows best when the time is right for "this matter."

Mufid wrote several treatises on the subject. He realized that the objections of rationalist theologians, who strove to show that Imami doctrine was contrary to reason, could not be dealt with effectively on the basis of traditional sources and simple interpretations of them. He introduced new arguments based on reason, and those became the basis for more systematic treatments of the doctrine at the hands of his pupils from the next generation of Imami scholars.

Proof of Existence of the Twelfth Imam

Opponents in the time of Mufid would attempt to discredit the traditional evidence adduced by Imamis as proof of the existence of the twelfth imam, on the basis that there is disagreement about his existence among Muslims and that the relevant reports have been transmitted within Imamism only. They would also argue that it is rationally impossible for the Mahdi to be still alive after so many years (145 years, according to one interlocutor).

Mufid defended the authenticity of the Imami Hadith reports by arguing that they have been transmitted by many Imamis from diverse backgrounds and different locations, all of whom knew that telling lies was sinful and could not have conspired to tell a lie. Moreover, if one were to insist on transmission by both advocate and opponent as a necessary criterion of authenticity, then one would have to reject all traditional sources and with it the whole basis of Islamic belief and doctrine and, indeed, the bases of all religions. In his defense of the hidden imam's prolonged life, Mufid relied mainly on the argument adduced by his teacher Ibn Babuya, namely, that many biblical and other figures were known to have lived very long lives and, hence, that the case of the Mahdi was not exceptional or contrary to reason.

Mufid also provided what he regarded as positive rational proof for the existence of the twelfth imam, though, in fact, his starting-point was the Imami tradition that "the earth can never be devoid of divine Proof." He argued that God's Proof can only be someone who is infallible, and since one can see that none of the 'Abbasids or 'Alids (viz., of those who have claimed the imamate) has this quality, it follows that the real Proof must be someone else and in hiding. This reasoning became the basis on which Mufid's pupil, the 'Alid Sharif Murtada, and later Imamis constructed their arguments.

Belief in the Invisible

One of the most common objections against the doctrine of occultation was that it contradicted the Imami belief in the necessity of the imamate and the obligation to know the imam of the time. Or, as one objector put it: how can one know and believe in the existence of someone who is never seen by ordinary mortals? Mufid explained that the necessity of the imamate does not entail that the imam be visible or not absent. Moreover, knowing things and believing in them does not depend solely on seeing them or experiencing them. We believe in things that happened in the past and things that will happen in the future, for example, the resurrection, without having personal experience of them. As to the purpose of acknowledging a hidden imam, Mufid did not provide an argument from reason. His answer was that knowing the imam fulfills an obligation imposed on us by God and brings us the benefit of reward and avoidance of punishment.

The Purpose of the Imam's Existence in Occultation

Another objector could not understand what practical purpose was served by the continued existence of the imam, given that he was unavailable to carry out his duties.

Mufid's answer was that the occultation of the imam does not preclude the community's need for him as guardian of the law and faith. Although the imam does not need to be in charge of everything himself and may appoint deputies who carry out his administrative duties, preach his message, and act as leaders in holy war, no one can take over his role as guardian of the law. As long as his followers are observing his and the other imams' teachings he may remain silent and in hiding. If, however, he finds them abandoning his traditions and going astray, then he must appear and take charge of their guidance personally.

In his justification of the occultation Mufid often argued on the basis of the theological principle that God acts only in the best interests of men, which is Mu'tazili in origin. (When Mufid spoke of "best interests," more often than not he had in mind the believers, not mankind in general.) But opponents could question whether God's decision to bring about the occultation can be said to be in man's best interests, given that evil could follow from it. Mufid's answer was that God is not the one to blame if the world becomes full of evil as a result of the occultation of the imam and the fact that he is not available to impose the legal penalties or to execute legal decisions. The blame, rather, is on the oppressors whom the imam feared when he went into occultation. Had God caused the imam to die and evil resulted from this, the blame would be on Him, but this is not the case.

Reasons for his Non-appearance

The principle of "best interests" was also invoked by Mufid when he addressed the objection that there is no good reason for the imam not to appear at least to his trusted disciples. He reasoned that the reward for believing in the hidden imam is greater than what one would gain were he visible, for it is harder to believe in an imam who is not visible and concerning whom there are many uncertainties. The imam knows that belief in him entails a greater effort and brings a greater reward, and so he is obliged to remain hidden.

But if the imam's occultation is deemed to be in the best interests of his followers, would it not follow that his appearance will be less good for them? Mufid disagreed, and explained that interests change with changing circumstances but they do not necessarily increase and decrease according to opposite circumstances. Thus, for example, if Imamis begin to act sinfully or disbelieve because of the prolongation of the imam's absence from them then God will make him appear in order to spare them the punishment they deserve. Sparing them the punishment and helping them to remain faithful is better for them than the reward they might have gained for believing in the hidden imam under different circumstances.

The argument that the imam went into occultation because of fear of oppressors was an old one. It had been used by Imamis since the late third/ninth century when it was first proclaimed that a successor of the eleventh imam existed and had gone into hiding. With the advent of the pro-Shi'i Buyids, when conditions would have appeared to be favorable for the appearance of the imam, that argument was ceasing to carry conviction among the faithful and was becoming increasingly difficult to maintain against the polemical attacks of outsiders. A main objection now was that the Mahdi's predecessors did not go into hiding even though they were persecuted, and now that the situation was much safer, there is no reason for him to remain in hiding.

Mufid dealt with this objection by recourse to the argument that the imam's predecessors had been in less danger than he is. It was well known, he says, that they had no intention of taking up arms against the rulers, whereas it has always been known that the twelfth imam would undertake that task. Therefore, if he appears now and this becomes known to his enemies before he is ready to launch his revolt, he would encounter hostility and resistance and this might jeopardize the successful outcome of his revolt. A similar argument had been used by Ibn Babuya.

A Mu'tazili is said to have raised the objection that if it is true the imam remained in hiding because of fear of his enemies, there is nothing to prevent him from appearing to his followers. Mufid responded by saying that the imam's followers are not infallible, hence, if they knew his whereabouts some of them might be tempted to reveal this to the authorities in the hope of worldly remuneration.

During another debating session one opponent pointed out to Mufid that the Imami tradition ascribes to the sixth imam, Ja'far al-Sadiq, the prediction that the Mahdi will appear as soon as three hundred men, the number of those who fought with the Prophet at the battle of Badr in Arabia, are available to join his uprising. And since there are now many more Imamis than that, the Mahdi must appear. To this Mufid replied that the men available today are not of the same caliber in courage and determination as those who fought at Badr. If three hundred such men become available and God and the Mahdi know that their rising will be successful, then the Mahdi will appear. Mufid justified his interpretation of Ja'far's statement on the basis that the number of warriors was not the only consideration for the Prophet in his decision whether or not to fight. On one occasion (during the episode known as Hudaybiyya) the Prophet decided not to fight his Meccan opponents even though he had with him many more men than he had at the battle of Badr.

Proof of the Mahdi's Identity

A Mu'tazili opponent is said to have objected that if the Mahdi appeared when none of those who could have seen him during his lesser occultation was still alive, he would have to provide proof of his identity. And since miracles are exclusively a sign of prophecy and the imam is not a prophet, he would have no means of proving his identity. Mufid's reply was that reports from the imams indicate that his appearance will be accompanied by many other signs, such as the appearance of the Impostor (the Muslim Antichrist) and the killing of the 'Alid Hasanid who will appear in Medina proclaiming the advent of the imam of the time. These signs are in themselves miracles which will occur "by his hands" (viz., they will be created by God through his intermediacy) and by which his lineage and his claim will be authenticated.

Mufid went on to say, against the Mu'tazili view, that miracles do not necessarily prove that the one who works them is a prophet. Rather, they serve to authenticate that person's claims, be he a prophet, an imam, or a pious believer calling upon people to recognize the prophethood of a prophet or the imamate of an imam. (This view of the function of miracles was in clear contrast to the view of Sunni theologians that miracles given to people other than prophets, for example, to mystic saints, must be kept secret and are not intended to prove their claims.) He also pointed to Qur'anic accounts according to which biblical figures, who were not prophets, were given miracles: Jesus' mother Mary was miraculously provided with food from heaven (Q. 3: 37), and Moses' mother received revelations concerning the infant Moses (Q. 28: 7). This evidence suggests to Mufid that the appearance of signs or miracles is also possible for the Mahdi and would prove his identity and distinguish him from other claimants.

5

THEOLOGY

According to a common view among modern scholars of Shi'ism, Imami theology underwent radical change at the hands of Mufid. He is thought to have been responsible for introducing Mu'tazili concepts and methods of reasoning on a scale unknown before in Imamism. Imami theology is said to have developed at his hands from a largely traditionalist and determinist stance to one that was anti-determinist and more open to rationalist ideas.

In more recent years, however, aspects of this view of the early development of Imami theology have been called into question, and a strong case has been presented for a more gradual and continuous line of development going back to the latter part of the third/ninth century, when Mu'tazili dogmas and concepts were beginning to gain acceptance among Imami Hadith scholars and theologians alike. Further, Mufid has been shown to have been more influenced by traditionalist Imami dogma than previously thought. With regard to the role of reason as a source of religious knowledge and a means of interpreting revelation, Mufid represented a halfway position between the traditionalist opponents of reason and the rationalist theologians who came to dominate later Imami thought.

Study of Mufid's theology highlights the fact that in Imamism the doctrine of the imamate remained central and prevented a complete assimilation of the Mu'tazili doctrine of divine justice. As we shall see, Mufid rejected the Mu'tazili doctrine of the unconditional and permanent punishment of the believing grave sinner and upheld the doctrine of intercession of the Prophet and the imams. This remained the position of all later Imami theologians.

MU'TAZILI THEOLOGY

The Mu'tazila had risen to a position of importance as a result of the interest in theological debate that emerged at the 'Abbasid court in Baghdad at the end of the second/eighth century. This was a time when more of the Near Eastern élite were beginning to convert to Islam and a need was felt to defend the faith and to define what it stood for and where it differed from the other religions. The Mu'tazila were not the only participants in those debates, but they were distinguished by their skill in the dialectical method (kalam) which they perfected and imbued with Greek philosophical concepts and modes of reasoning. (Kalam means "speech" or "discourse." The term was used by early Muslims to denote both theology and the dialectical method favored by its practitioners, where objections and responses to them were given in the form "If they say ..., we say to them ... .") The aim of the Mu'tazila was to replace the crude and popular conception of God that prevailed among early Muslims with a more rational one which reduced His arbitrary power and stressed His justice and absolute uniqueness.

The Mu'tazila and the Role of Reason

Against the dominant trend in early Islam, the Mu'tazila held that human reason, and not revelation, was the primary basis of man's knowledge of God. Reason enables man to establish all the basic truths about God – that He exists and that He is creator, all powerful, and omniscient. Reason is also the source of knowledge of good and evil. We are capable of knowing by our reason alone that deceit and injustice are wrong, or that repaying a debt is obligatory. This means that man would be under moral obligation to do right even if there were no prophets.

The primacy of reason did not mean, however, that revelation is superfluous. On the contrary, its aim is to help man in choosing what is right. God is in fact obliged to send prophets for He must do what is in man's best interests. Thus, revelation confirms the results of rational investigation and must be interpreted in accordance with the dictates of reason. Any contradiction between the Qur'an and rational theology is only apparent and could be resolved through appropriate interpretation of the texts. The Mu'tazila also recognized that it is only through revelation that man knows about God's imposition of certain laws and rituals, for example, the five-times daily prayer and the prohibition on eating pork, and about things such as punishment and reward and the resurrection of the dead before the Day of Judgment.

Unity

The Mu'tazila called themselves the people of "Justice and Unity." This dual principle was the basis on which their whole system was built. Regarding divine unity, they emphasized its absoluteness, which, in the first place, meant a strict monotheism as opposed to Manichaean dualism and Christian Trinitarianism. Unity in this sense was an essential postulate for all Muslims. For the Mu'tazila it also meant the transcendence and uniqueness of God, that He is beyond time and space, unchangeable and incorporeal (or not composed of matter). They described their position as against corporealism and anthropomorphism (the likening of God to His creatures) and in favor of transcendentalism. To support their position they adduced the Qur'anic statement that "nothing resembles Him," and they insisted that the seemingly anthropomorphic expressions applied to God in the Qur'an, for example, those which speak of God's hand and face, must be understood metaphorically as references to His power and grace.

In elaborating their doctrine of unity the Mu'tazila addressed the question of how the names or attributes given to God in the Qur'an may be understood without any suggestion of a composite nature. The solutions they came up with, and many of the concepts they used, had parallels in Christian discussions about the nature of Jesus and his relationship to God. They spoke of two kinds of attributes. They said that the attributes of power, knowledge, and life are identical with the divine essence, not different entities, because nothing can be co-eternal with God. As for God's willing, seeing, and speaking, these are attributes of act. They are created by Him outside his essence and are subject to change; they cease to exist when He stops acting.

This anti-anthropomorphism of the Mu'tazila and their views on divine attributes were relevant to the position they took in a major controversy over the nature of the Qur'an, which erupted in the early third/ninth century, during the reign of the caliph Ma'mun (198/813–218/833). Like all Muslims, the Mu'tazila had come to regard the Qur'an as the "word" or speech of God. However, against the view of most other Muslims, they insisted that the Qur'an was *created* not *spoken* by God, because, as they said, God does not resemble mankind and does not have an organ of speech. They went on to assert that it is not eternal but created "in time."

Justice

The Muʿtazila tended to speak more commonly of "the five principles" as their distinctive theses than of "Justice and Unity." In fact, the other three principles may be regarded as components of their doctrine of justice.

According to their doctrine, God is necessarily just and good. He wills and does only that which is good; the "good" is what human reason recognizes to be so and is the same for God. Justice is not only a fact for God, it is also an obligation. It entails punishing the sinner, rewarding the good, pardoning the one who repents, and compensating those who do not merit the suffering that is sometimes inflicted by God as punishment on mankind.

Their principle of "the promise and the threat" referred to the promises of reward and the threats of punishment which God has made in the Qur'an. They said that the promise of eternal reward for the obedient believer (that is, the one who acts in accordance with the law and adheres to the basic dogmas of Islam), and the threat of eternal punishment for the unrepentant grave sinner, must be carried out by God on the Day of Judgment, otherwise evil would turn into good and good into evil and God would be failing to fulfill His promises. There can be no unmerited reward, unmerited punishment, or intercession on behalf of sinners. Only repenting sinners will benefit from the Prophet's intercession on the Day of Judgment. For some Muʿtazilis eternal punishment for the unrepentant grave sinner appeared to be inconsistent with divine justice, and so they opted for the milder idea of a long period in purgatory.

The unrepentant grave sinner was classified by the Muʿtazila as belonging to an "intermediate rank," meaning that he is neither a believer who deserves reward nor an unbeliever, since only a non-Muslim whose beliefs contradict the basic tenets of Islam could be described as an unbeliever. The Muslim grave sinner, like the unbeliever, certainly deserves eternal punishment, but the suffering of the Muslim will be less severe than that of the unbeliever.

Justice also necessitates that human beings have free choice, for it would be unjust of God to determine their acts and then punish them for committing sins or reward them for obedience. Men must be free to choose to believe or not to believe, and must be the producers of their own acts. But it is also necessary that God give them the help and the means to believe and to choose acts of obedience. The intelligence He gives them, the proofs by which He makes Himself known to them, and the revelation of His will through prophets are acts of divine favor (*lutf*), which help them and remove obstacles in the way of their choosing obedience. Also from His favor, God gives men the power (*qudra*) to produce or create their own acts, and He does not impose on them any obligation which they are unable to fulfill.

Everything God does is for the good of mankind. The aim of creating them and subjecting them to the law is to enable them to attain salvation. Indeed He always acts in the best interests of men's religion or future life. Some even said that God is obliged to do for men what is in the best interests of both their religion *and* their life on earth.

Another principle related to the doctrine of justice was that of "commanding the right and forbidding the wrong." This was a common precept in early Islam and referred to the duty of all Muslims to interfere publicly (and sometimes physically) in order to deter or stop bad behavior. In early Islam it included the duty to resist unjust rule. In later political theory, which was mostly quietist, the performance of the duty "with the hand," that is, by using force, was limited to the political authorities. As for performing it "with the tongue," or practising admonition, most Muslim scholars tended to assign a more prominent role to themselves than to other Muslims. Among the Mu'tazila the duty was connected with the concept of divine favor and regarded as helping man to choose obedience and a deterrent against disobedience.

Reactions against the Mu'tazila

The Mu'tazila encountered strong opposition over both their dogmas and their views on the role of reason, especially from traditionalist scholars. Scholars who derived their authority from studying and transmitting the revealed texts felt threatened by the idea that a large part of the law is discoverable by means of reason. Also relevant was the fact that many of those scholars owed their position in society to the support of the common people. The latter were more comfortable with the concept of a personal God who determines everything in this world, including human acts, and who is not restricted in His acts by any rules or principles.

Nevertheless, the influence of the Mu'tazila on the early development of Islamic theology was significant. Other sects and schools of theology were prompted to define their own positions on questions first raised by the Mu'tazila. Most were motivated to modify their anthropomorphic and determinist positions, and came up with compromise solutions. They also adopted some of the Mu'tazili tools of reasoning and used them to defend their own positions. Many of the Mu'tazili doctrines concerning divine attributes and justice were adopted in Zaydi Shi'ism and, as we shall see, in Imami Shi'ism.

SUNNI THEOLOGY

Reaction against the Mu'tazila culminated in the fourth/tenth century in the formulation, and eventually wide acceptance, of a rival Sunni theology. Its founder, Ash'ari, is reputed to have been a Mu'tazili before his conversion to Sunnism. His declared aim was to defend the doctrine of Sunni traditionalists, but in fact his system included some modification of their positions.

Ash'ari based his theological conclusions mostly on the Qur'an and Hadith, and he espoused the traditionalist view that revelation was the only basis of our knowledge of good and evil. Yet his theology remained suspect in the eyes of Sunni traditionalists because he relied on *kalam*-style argumentation and, when the revealed sources failed him, he would often base his reasoning on the common human experience.

According to the Ash'ari system, God is completely free in His acts towards mankind. He chooses to guide some people and to lead others astray, exactly as the Qur'an says. He punishes and rewards whom He wishes and as He wishes. The Mu'tazili position concerning justice was rejected as tantamount to subjecting God to human rules. God is certainly just, but not on the basis of human criteria. Whatever He does is just, even if He were to do the opposite. He does not act only for the welfare of mankind. And He alone knows the purpose behind the imposition of laws. There are, in other words, no restrictions on His power and it is not man's job to look for motives in any divine action or command.

Man does not have free will or the power to create his own acts because God is the creator of everything, yet God is not responsible for man's sinful acts. The difficulty was resolved on the basis that God creates in man the power to act at the moment of action but it is man who "acquires" (*kasb*) the responsibility for his own acts. For Ash'ari's Mu'tazili opponents this made no sense at all; they could not see how man can be responsible for acts that he does not himself create.

On the question of faith, the Ash'aris, contrary to the Mu'tazila, put the emphasis on internal conviction and did not regard works as an integral part of faith. Works are merely the perfection of faith or, more accurately, good works enhance and sins diminish the quality of faith, not faith itself. Every Muslim, regardless of his sins (polytheism and denying the Prophet excepted), is a believer and will ultimately be saved from eternal hell, as the Prophet will intercede for all Muslims on the Day of Resurrection. That is not to say that sinners will escape all punishment. According to most Muslims, but not according to the Mu'tazila, punishment and reward begin to take place "in the grave," that is, in the interval between death and the Day of Resurrection.

The Ash'aris also rejected the Mu'tazili doctrine of unity and affirmed the existence in God of eternal attributes. Denying their existence, they said, would lead to denying the very existence of God. In line with this they held that the Qur'an, as the speech of God, is uncreated and eternal. Against accusations of anthropomorphism, they adopted the view that God's attributes do not resemble those of humans but that their nature is beyond human comprehension. Their reality must be accepted without questioning or, as Ash'ari theologians would often say when the revealed sources proved to be irreconcilable with reason, "without asking how."

EARLY IMAMISM BETWEEN REASON AND REVELATION

As discussed briefly in the Introduction, early Imamism was characterized by a predominantly traditionalist outlook. However, it did not have the same aversion to the methods or subject-matter of *kalam* found among Sunni traditionalists. This requires some explanation.

In theory, and because of the recognized position of the imams as the sole authorities on all religious matters, we would expect Imamis to have regarded as superfluous and subject to error all theological speculations and attempts to discover religious truths through use of reasoning and analysis. In reality, Imami scholars are known to have participated in the theological debates of their time and, as the evidence of reports and extant fragments suggests, there were certainly elements of rational thinking in their polemical and apologetic writings. One might conclude from this that by engaging in theological debates and expressing views on various questions of dogma, Imami scholars were not being true to their own doctrine of the imamate. But this was not how it would have seemed to them, or how they would have presented their position.

In the early development of Imami theology, whether one cited the views of the imams or not, the assumption always was that theological formulations and arguments were based on their teachings and not arrived at independently by the scholars themselves. This view of the science of *kalam* (or the science of divine unity, as Imamis preferred to call it), that it formed part of the legacy of the imams, is reflected in the fact that articles of dogma, as well as the reasoning adduced to support them, appeared in the form of Hadith reports from the imams. If in their discussions with other theologians early Imami scholars are not known to have cited the teachings and views of the imams but presented their theological positions as based on reasoning and analysis, this is explicable on the basis that Imami dogma developed in the course of polemical encounters with opponents who did not recognize the teachings of the imams as valid arguments in theology. As Imamis (or most of them) would have seen it, *kalam* was a means of defending their dogma, not for deriving it. Moreover, the use of *kalam* for defensive purposes was said to have had the imams' approval.

This traditionalism became increasingly difficult to maintain after the disappearance of the last imam and the severance of all contact with his community. The existing body of Imami Hadith might have incorporated much of the developments in law and theology that had taken place over the previous two centuries. But it was no longer sufficient to meet the demands of a polemically engaged sect and a developing law and theology. Scholars who recognized that the traditionalist position was putting Imamism at a disadvantage were beginning to explore ways of widening the basis of Imami doctrine and to admit a role for reason and interpretation.

It is often suggested in modern studies that these early attempts in the direction of rationalization, which appeared in the post-occultation period, were from the beginning strongly opposed by other Imamis eager to preserve the traditionalist character of the sect. There is, however, no good evidence for the existence of such opposition, or of conflict between advocates and opponents of reason, before the second half of the fourth/tenth century. Its absence before then may be explained on the basis that the focus of Imami scholarship and of much of its polemical encounters with opponents was still on the imamate and the occultation, and not on theology proper. Also, initially the introduction of new rational arguments proceeded slowly, and these could still be presented as implicit in the teachings of the imams.

With the advent in 334/945 of the Shi'i Buyid dynasty, who were great patrons of religious learning, there was, as we have said, an upsurge of interest in theological debate between the various sects and schools. Imamis now found themselves under increasing pressure to define their positions in a more systematic fashion and to demonstrate that they are not contrary to reason or, even, that they can be proved by reason. The modest steps that had already been taken in the direction of rationalization were now beginning to accelerate. It was against this background that the Qummi scholar Ibn Babuya launched his attacks on *kalam*.

Ibn Babuya came from and received his religious education in the Iranian city of Qumm. The city had been a main center for the transmission and collection of Imami Hadith since the middle of the third century, and was now becoming a center of opposition to the emerging rationalist tendencies within Imamism. Ibn Babuya expressed open hostility to theological debate and disputation especially when engaged in by those who are not well versed in it. The imams, he claimed, forbade it, and allowed it only to the learned. Even the learned theologian had to limit himself to citing the Qur'an and the sayings of the Prophet and the imams and explaining their meaning. In his own theological works Ibn Babuya relied almost exclusively on traditional sources and simple explanations of them. In his view *kalam* as a theological discipline was superfluous; all the necessary rational arguments had been formulated by the imams themselves and may be found in Hadith reports from them.

Paradoxically, Ibn Babuya seems to have been willing at times to concede that human reason was a valid means of inquiring into matters of law and dogma. In fact, on a number of occasions he actually adduces rational arguments used by other jurists and by theologians on the question of the imamate. This ambivalent attitude to the role of reason and the reluctance to use it himself may have been as much determined by a lack of adequate training in rational theology as it was by his declared conviction that its undisciplined use would result in confusion and failure to present a coherent exposition and defense of Imami doctrine. Be that as it may, his views were severely criticized by Mufid who argued in favor of a role for reason and defended the use of *kalam*.

MUFID AND THE ROLE OF REASON

Mufid denied that the imams had prohibited their disciples from engaging in religious discussions. He argued that the Hadith reports adduced by Ibn Babuya were injunctions not against *kalam per se* but against attributing to God injustice and anthropomorphic forms and characteristics. (A similar understanding of the imams' position on *kalam* may be inferred from Kulini's *Kafi*, where the prohibition against *kalam* is not general but specific to speculating on the "nature" of God, meaning His form and what He is composed of.) Mufid also pointed to reports according to which the imams explicitly encouraged disciples who were well grounded in their teachings to engage in *kalam*, and he noted that many leading Imamis from that time were, in fact, known to have participated in such discussions. It is through *kalam*, he tells us, that a learned believer is able to defend Imami beliefs, repel falsehood, and confound opponents.

His position concerning the admissibility of *kalam* did not however entail recognition of reason as a source of doctrine. Unlike the Mu'tazila who believed that theological and juristic conclusions may be drawn from reason, Mufid regarded it as essentially a means of constructing arguments for defending doctrines which have already been established by revelation. As he put it, reason needs revelation in order to attain certitude.

The primacy that he assigns to revelation is apparent everywhere in his work, even when he discusses the "finer matters of theology," for which there are no references in the Qur'an or in Hadith. In discussing these questions he would often base his acceptance of a doctrine not on positive rational argument but on whether that doctrine is compatible with other revealed doctrines. For example, he accepts the physical theory of the "four elements" (heat, cold, humidity, and dryness) on the basis that there is no valid argument against it and that it does not contradict anything of the doctrines of justice, unity, prophecy, or of the revealed law. Sometimes he accepts a Mu'tazili position on the basis that the theory and the reasoning behind it are sound, but then denies its validity on the grounds that it is contrary to revealed knowledge. For example, reason tells us that someone who murders a believer and considers it licit to do so can one day repent and become a believer. But Hadith tells us that such a person will never repent.

Hadith Criticism

Like earlier Imami scholars, Mufid was aware that to be able to maintain that all dogma was based on the Qur'an and Hadith one had to deal with contradictory statements within Hadith, or between Hadith and Qur'an. In the time of Kulini and Ibn Babuya there were already reports from the imams which instructed the faithful in the right procedures for determining the authenticity of Hadith reports from them. For example, Imamis were told to compare the imams' statements with the Qur'an: if they agreed with it then they are authentic, otherwise they must be discarded as false.

Mufid went further in his approach to the study of Hadith. Concerning the question of authenticity, the decisive criterion for him was whether a report has been transmitted by multiple witnesses or through several channels. In fact most Muslim scholars had come to believe that widely attested reports yielded certitude. The reasoning behind this was that a large number of people cannot possibly become involved in fabricating and spreading reports without this becoming known to others. Thus, Mufid would often reject Hadith reports adduced by Ibn Babuya in support of his theological positions, on the grounds that those reports were not widely attested. He would accept isolated reports only if they could be supported by another proof such as a rational argument, a Qur'anic text, or the consensus of the Imamiyya or of the whole community.

As we have seen in Chapter 4, Mufid invoked the concept of "wide attestation" against opponents who argued that reports about the Imami imamate were transmitted within Imamism only and, therefore, did not constitute valid proof. He had two strategies for dealing with such objections: the first was based on the idea of attestation outside Shi'ism, and the second on the reliability of Imami transmitters. Thus he tried to show, for example, that reports from the Prophet about 'Ali's imamate had also been transmitted outside Shi'ism but that they were misinterpreted or rejected by opponents of the 'Alids. However, where such a definition of "wide attestation" was not possible, as for example in the case of reports about miracles by the imams, transmitted within Imamism only, Mufid would sometimes fall back on the argument that those transmitters were known for their honesty and reliability, and that the eye-witnesses among them did not all know each other and hence they could not have conspired to falsify the reports.

But for Mufid it was not sufficient to determine the authenticity of Hadith reports. It was also essential to interpret correctly all Hadith and Qur'anic statements on matters of dogma. These statements must not always be understood literally. Some must be understood metaphorically, and it is always necessary to interpret them in accordance with well-established knowledge. In practice, this meant that Hadith statements which did not agree with his own theological positions, and which, for other reasons, he could not reject as inauthentic, were often interpreted away. Other epistemological questions that Mufid grappled with, and which were relevant mainly to legal theory, will be discussed in the next chapter.

Thus, whereas for the Mu'tazila reason was the primary source of religious knowledge and provided proofs for the veracity of the revelation, for Mufid reason was a means of defending traditional doctrines and of evaluating and inter-preting traditions. In this respect his influence on later Imamism was limited, as his pupils, who dominated the field in the next generation, came to accept fully the Mu'tazili view that reason was the essential basis for constructing theology.

THE DOGMAS OF IMAMISM

We shall now consider the content of Imami theology and Mufid's contribution to its development. The earliest Imami theologians who flourished in the late second/eighth century held views which mostly contrasted with those of their Mu'tazili contemporaries and did not differ much from those adopted by Sunni traditionalists. Their views were essentially anthropomorphist and determinist, and consistent with literal interpretations of Qur'anic statements about God, in contrast to the Mu'tazila who held that such statements must be understood metaphorically. Thus, early Imamis spoke of the visibility of God and said that He is located on His throne, that He moves (descends to the lower heavens and returns to the throne), and that He controls all events in the world including the acts of men.

In the face of severe criticism by the Mu'tazila, and perhaps also out of a desire to formulate distinctive Imami dogma, there soon arose attempts to modify the traditional and largely anthropomorphic conceptions of God, and to find intermedi-ate positions between Sunni and Mu'tazili dogmas, in questions such as free will versus predestination and the divine attributes. These intermediate positions were often expressed in the form of short statements by (or, perhaps, ascribed to) the imams. Thus, the statement that "the Qur'an is the speech of God, neither creator nor created" expressed a rejection of the position which said that the Qur'an is "uncreated" and implied that it is identical with the creator, as well as the Mu'tazili doctrine of its createdness. According to another early Imami formulation, "the attributes are neither God, nor other than God," meaning that, contrary to the view of the Mu'tazila, they are not identical with His essence and, contrary to the view of Sunni theologians, they are not separate eternal entities; rather, they are to be understood as existing "in God." On the question of whether the acts of men are created by God, early Imamis expressed their position as "neither compulsion nor delegation," meaning that God neither compels man to disobedience, as Sunni doctrine implied, nor delegates to him the power to create his own acts, as the Mu'tazila said.

By the later third/ninth century, Imami theology had come to incorporate a number of Mu'tazili concepts and formulations. This is attested in the extant Hadith collections and in reports about the views and works of Imami theologians from this period. The noteworthy feature of this theology is that in questions pertaining to divine unity it now agreed very closely with the abstract conception of God taught by the Mu'tazila. In questions pertaining to divine justice, on the other hand, significant differences with Mu'tazili doctrine remained. Mufid, as we shall see, moved a few steps closer than his predecessors towards Mu'tazili doctrine but crucial differences remained. In fact, in view of the position that the imamate occupied in Imami belief and its role in salvation, a complete assimilation of the Mu'tazili theodicy was never achieved in Imamism.

Unity

Examination of the views of Imami theologians and Hadith scholars shows that by the late third/ninth century, if not earlier, most Imamis had come to reject anthropomorphic and corporealist conceptions of God. They had also come to adopt the Mu'tazili doctrine of attributes with its distinction between the attributes of essence and the attributes of act. The older intermediate position which said that "the attributes are neither God nor other than God" was superseded by the (essentially Mu'tazili) view that the eternal attributes are identical with the divine essence, not real entities exisiting within it. Thus, God was said to be eternally knowing by His essence and not by a knowledge which is separate from it, and the same was said of the attributes "living," "powerful," "hearing," and "seeing." Mufid did not add much to this except to say that "hearing" and "seeing" are part of "knowledge." He also tried to explain that the names given to divine attributes reflect men's conception of the divine reality and not that reality itself.

The Qur'an as the Speech of God. Also like the Mu'tazila, Imamis had come to regard "speaking" and "willing" as attributes of act and created in time. A related development concerned their position on the nature of the Qur'an as the word/speech of God. The earlier intermediate position expressed in the formulation "neither creator nor created" was superseded by the doctrine of its createdness/temporality. This development presented Imamis with a problem, since the earlier formulation had been closely associated with the imams and Imami scholars from that period and, hence, could not be easily rejected as inauthentic or insufficiently attested. But it could be reinterpreted and harmonized with the new doctrine.

Imami Hadith reports indicate that Imamis achieved this by using a different term to describe the temporality of the attributes of act: they said they are "produced in time" and refused to call them "created." The specific problem of the nature of the Qur'an, and how to reconcile the idea of its temporality with the imams' statement that it was "not created," was dealt with by Ibn Babuya. He explained that when the imams said "not created" they meant not fabricated or fictitious; they did not mean to say it was not produced in time. Mufid took a similar view, and presented his position as based on the traditions of the imams. Like Ibn Babuya, he insisted on using the term "produced in time" and refused to say "created."

Bada' or Change of Divine Decree. Highly objectionable from the Mu'tazili and Sunni points of view was the Imami doctrine of bada', or the idea that it is possible for God to change His will in response to changing circumstances. In the Imami tradition the doctrine was associated with the sixth imam, Ja'far, and his designation of his son Isma'il as the next imam. It was said that when Isma'il died prematurely during his father's lifetime, his father explained to his followers that God had changed his will (bada) concerning Isma'il's imamate, and he went on to designate his son Musa as the next imam. In the Hadith sources there are a number of reports in favor of the doctrine. For example, the imams are said to have taught that "God is glorified by nothing so much as by the belief in bada'."

Opponents of the Imamis accused their imams of adducing bada' in order to justify the non fulfillment of the predictions they had made to their followers. The doctrine was also criticized because it had implications of divine ignorance; it implied that God may decree one thing and later its opposite on the basis of new knowledge which He did not have before. These criticisms could not be ignored by Imami theologians. Already in the late third/ninth century some Imamis were arguing that *bada'* is essentially the same as the doctrine of abrogation (*naskh*) in law, which all Muslims accepted. They said that *bada'* entails commanding different things at different times; it does not entail any change in divine knowledge. There were also attempts to reinterpret the doctrine in ways that would remove those aspects which outsiders found so offensive, in particular, the idea of God acquiring new knowledge.

According to Ibn Babuya, one aspect of *bada'* is effectively the same as abrogation in religious law. Another aspect is that God is free in His actions, that He may decide to make things happen sooner or later. *Bada'* also means that He responds to the free actions of men, for example, by increasing or decreasing the term of a man's life in accordance with his behavior. This concept would have been acceptable to the Mu'tazila as they themselves had taught a similar doctrine about God's changing of a man's life span. Similar arguments in defense of the doctrine of *bada'*, and with the aim of harmonizing it with God's eternal knowledge, were made by Mufid.

All these arguments did not, however, resolve the difficulty implied in the tradition about Ja'far's designation of Isma'il and the latter's premature death. For if God revealed to Ja'far that Isma'il would be his successor, and then Isma'il died and God made another revelation concerning Musa (the seventh imam), the implication remains that when He revealed His will concerning Isma'il, God did not know that Isma'il would die before his father. Mufid attempted to resolve the problem linguistically by arguing, on the basis of Qur'anic usage, that *bada'* means appearance, and that it is appearance to men not to God. Thus, when Imam Ja'far used the term in connection with Isma'il's death he meant that something unexpected appeared to him from God's hand, not that God had changed his mind about Isma'il.

Justice

By the late third/ninth century Imami theology had come to agree with Mu'tazili theology on the basic principles of divine justice. God does only good. He does not act wrongly or arbitrarily, although He could do so if He wished. By revealing His commands and prohibitions He provides man with guidance towards good and away from wrong. He does not lay on man any obligation that he cannot fulfill. He gives him the necessary knowledge, help, and capability to fulfill His commands. He does not punish man except for sins he has committed, and He rewards good deeds. He compensates those who do not merit the suffering that He sometimes inflicts as punishment on mankind. In all these basic principles Mufid remained close to the views attested among his predecessors and in Hadith sources.

God's Acts and Man's Best Interests. Imami Hadith scholars and Ibn Babuya spoke of God's acts as always just and good. Their statements suggest, however, that, unlike the Mu'tazila, they conceived of God as acting first and foremost for the welfare of believers (viz., Imamis), not of every individual. What is not clear is whether for them, as for the Mu'tazila, God's acts are *always* in man's best interests.

On this latter question Mufid adopted the same position as the Mu'tazila. He stated clearly that God always does for His servants what is in their best interests, both in this world and in the next. But he was not entirely consistent. Although in principle he held that every one (including unbelievers) must benefit from God's acts, he, like his predecessors, was concerned with the effects of God's actions on believers only. This is reflected, for example, in his view concerning the doctrine of compensation. Whereas the Mu'tazila, as we have seen, taught that men are owed compensation if God causes them unmerited pain from which they themselves receive no gain, for Mufid unbelievers are not owed compensation. The same lack of concern with unbelievers is reflected in his treatment of the problem of why, given that God created man for salvation, He did not create him in Paradise from the start. (In the Muslim tradition the heavenly Paradise is usually distinguished from the Eden of Adam – an earthly Garden.) Mufid argued that God could not have created man in Paradise, and without subjecting him to any trial on earth, because He had to give the righteous believer the possibility of earning a greater reward.

Mufid agreed with the Mu'tazila that God's imposition on mankind of commands and prohibitions, subjecting them to a law, is for their own good. The imposition of a law affords them the best chance of salvation and through its fulfillment earns them reward in the afterlife. As to how man acquires the knowledge that God has laid on him obligations, Mufid's view was different from the Mu'tazili. For the Mu'tazila the obligations are known in two ways: by our reason which tells us, for example, that it is good to be kind and truthful, and to be thankful to a benefactor; and by revelation through which we know the specific obligations. For Mufid, on the other hand, man gets to know the obligations only through the revelation that a prophet brings and through its interpretation by an imam whom God appoints as teacher after the death of the prophet.

On the question of God's responsibility for the evil in this world, the position taken by Mufid was not too far removed from that attested in the traditional sources and advocated by his predecessor Ibn Babuya, although it might appear to be. According to those sources, God being all powerful, everything good and bad happens by His will. But they do not mean to say thereby that God is responsible for, or that he prompts, the evil acts of men. Nor do they mean that He Himself commits, or is free to commit, evil acts. On the contrary, they, like Mufid, deny this and insist that He always acts for the good. What they actually mean is that God "allows" evil acts to take place in the sense that He does not interfere to stop them. Mufid's position was essentially the same except that his starting-point was that God is free from all evil, whereas the traditionalists started from the premise of His power.

Man's Power of Choice. As mentioned already, one of the early Imami positions on whether the acts of men are determined by God was expressed in the dictum "neither compulsion nor delegation." This amounted to saying that, contrary to Sunni doctrine, God does not compel man to disobedience and, contrary to Mu'tazili doctrine, He does not delegate to him the power to create his own acts. (The Sunnis themselves would have objected to the description of their position as "compulsionist." On their doctrine of "acquisition (*kasb*)," see above the section entitled "Sunni theology.") Other statements found in Hadith sources also suggest that early Imamis tried to avoid formulations that might appear to diminish the absolute power of God or, conversely, to make Him responsible for everything including the evil acts of men. Thus, it was said that nothing in the world happens if God does not allow it to happen and men can never act against the will of God. Yet God does not have a direct influence over men's acts, and they are free to choose to obey or to disobey.

These early Imami attempts to resolve the question of free will in view of divine omnipotence drew on the essentially Mu'tazili doctrine of man's ability to act in relation to the act. According to this doctrine, it is God who gives man the ability for a particular act, but this ability comes a moment before the act leaving man free to choose between two alternatives, between one act and its opposite. Also as in Mu'tazilism, Imami

Hadith reports spoke of the ability to act as dependent on physical aptitude. But although man was seen to have free choice and, effectively, to be the producer of his own acts, early Imamis, unlike the Mu'tazila, were generally reluctant to call man producer or creator of his own acts.

Mufid's teacher Ibn Babuya, whilst opposed to the idea of man as the producer of his own acts, also tried to argue that God's will does not force men to carry out particular acts. One of his solutions, for which he was criticized by Mufid, was that God creates the acts of men not by producing them but by pre-estimating them or creating them in His foreknowledge. Mufid rejected this solution and the Hadith report it is based on as inauthentic. He argued that pre-estimation is not foreknowledge but the same thing as creation, and it does not make any sense to distinguish the two concepts as Ibn Babuya did. He went on to cite other reports from the imams which say that man is the sole producer of his acts.

He also rejected Ibn Babuya's interpretation of the imam's statement "neither compulsion, nor delegation." According to Ibn Babuya, the statement meant that God neither commands man to perform an act of disobedience nor prevents him from performing it. In giving his own interpretation, Mufid is clear, as he is whenever he discusses this question, that God gives man the power to choose and to "produce" his own acts. He remained unwilling, however, to say that man "creates" his own acts, on the grounds that in the Qur'an the term is used only in connection with God.

On the specific question of whether God determines belief and unbelief, the Imami Hadith tradition exhibits more inconsistency than it does on the question of man's acts in general. One set of reports teaches, on the basis of Qur'anic statements, that men are created by God as believers or unbelievers. According to other reports, God does not force men to

believe; rather He urges them to choose right guidance, to follow the dictates of the revelation, and to believe in the imams
and adhere to their teachings. Both Ibn Babuya and Mufid built
their respective doctrines of free will on such statements. Both
felt obliged to interpret Qur'anic statements and Hadith
reports indicating predestination in ways contrary to those
envisaged by advocates of predestination. On one question,
however, Mufid contradicted his own doctrine of free will: he
accepted Hadith reports which said that children born of adul-
terous relationships can never be believers.

Faith and Salvation. Muslim theologians and jurists defined
faith as consisting of internal conviction, verbal confession (the
utterance of the formula that "there is no God but God and
Muhammad is His messenger"), and performance of works. In
Sunnism and in Imamism, the emphasis was on internal
conviction; good works were deemed to increase faith and
their omission to decrease it. For the Mu'tazila, the emphasis
was on works.

From an early stage Imamis drew a distinction between faith
and Islam: they held every believer to be a Muslim but not
every Muslim to be also a believer. At the heart of this distinction was the doctrine of the imamate and the idea that it is an
essential element of faith. Without recognition of, and devotion to, the imams there is no true belief. It is belief in the imamate, and not good works or the fulfillment of religious
obligations, that affords man the best chance of salvation; without it, all good works are of no avail in the afterlife.

Regarding the status of the grave sinner, Imamis rejected the
Mu'tazili doctrine of the intermediate position (that he is neither a Muslim nor an infidel) and insisted that he remains a
Muslim. As to his status as a believer, one of the early Imami
views was that a grave sinner "goes out of faith" when he

commits a sin and "goes back to faith" if he repents. Mufid took a different view: a believer who commits a grave sin is neither merely a believer nor merely a sinner but has aquired the status of sinful believer. This position was related to the way Mufid envisaged internal conviction. For him knowledge of God (that is, of His existence, unity, justice, and revelation to the Prophet) is not just a commitment that one makes in the heart, it is also intellectual knowledge. True faith is based on such clear understanding that once acquired it can never be lost or impaired. Obedience, good works, and repentance follow automatically from true knowledge and understanding of God.

On the fate of sinful believers, Mufid, like earlier Imamis, said they will all benefit from the intercession of the Prophet and the imams on the Day of Judgment and will be saved from eternal Hell. Only unbelievers will be punished in Hell forever and will not benefit from intercession. In Imami Hadith we find the idea that believers who commit sins receive their punishment in this life and go straight to Paradise after death. But according to Mufid, they may also have to undergo punishment and purification in the place known as the barzakh (a kind of purgatory), which he envisaged as separate from Hell, when they will be given life in temporary bodies. They will enter Paradise with their own resurrected bodies when the time of the Resurrection arrives.

Two points are worth noting here. Firstly, Mufid's doctrine that sinful believers will be given temporary bodies when they undergo purification in the barzakh is related to two other sets of ideas. One is his definition of the essence of man as spirit and immaterial, spirit being the life that inhabits the body. (A similar definition is attested for a number of earlier Imami theologians. The Mu'tazila, on the other hand, identified man as a body that has accidents of life, knowledge, and power. And the dominant Muslim doctrine was that man is both spirit and body, the spirit itself being a body though of a different nature from the sensible body.)

The other set of ideas concerns the doctrine known among Muslims (but rejected by the Mu'tazila) as the "torment of the grave." According to the most common version of this doctrine, when the body dies the soul departs for the first judgment then returns to the body for the questioning "in the grave" and remains there foretasting bliss or punishment until the Resurrection and the Last Judgment. Mufid accepted that the dead undergo examination in the grave but not that reward and punishment take place there; these take place in the Garden or in the place(s) of torment (Hell and the *barzakh*), depending on the belief status of the individual. He also accepted, along with the majority of Muslims, that punishment and reward are of both the spirit and the body. Therefore, since the essence of man is spirit, God can give him a temporary body in which he can be rewarded or punished in the time between death and the Resurrection.

The second point to note is that within the framework of a theology that emphasized divine justice, punishment after death for the sinful (Imami) believer, such as that envisaged by Mufid, might appear to fit in better than the idea of no punishment and direct entry into Paradise, such as that advocated by other Imamis and attested in Hadith. But the difference between the two positions is not really that significant. For Mufid, as for other Imamis, it remained the case that men's acts were largely irrelevant to their ultimate and eternal fate and that faith, with its essential constituent of loyalty to the imams, was the real key to salvation.

Raj'a or Return to Life. An important component of Imami belief about the afterlife was the doctrine of return (*raj'a*) to life of some of the dead before the Day of Resurrection. This, it was believed, will be during the age of the Mahdi, when God will restore to life some of the best believers (including one or more of the imams, according to some versions) and some of their worst enemies. He will give the believers victory and revenge over their opponents. They will then all die to await the Resurrection and eternal reward or punishment.

The doctrine remained a subject of dispute between Imamis and their opponents. The Mu'tazila saw in it a contradiction of divine justice. One of the arguments they used against Imamis was that if people knew that they would come back to life and that they would be given the chance to repent and escape punishment, this would entice them to commit acts of disobedience in this life. It may be due to objections of this nature that some Imamis reinterpreted the doctrine of *raj'a* as the "return of power" to the Shi'a at the hands of the Mahdi. This view, however, was rejected by Mufid and other scholars of the Buyid period. In response to similar objections by a Mu'tazili, Mufid argued that although it is rationally possible that those unbelievers will repent of their deeds, there are well attested traditions from the imams indicating that God would not accept their repentance and that they will be in Hell for ever. The Mu'tazili retorted that if this were so, the return would be an enticement for the unbelievers to do more evil after their return, since they would know that their repentance would not be accepted in any case. Mufid's reply was that their past experience of punishment would teach them not to want to incur more of it by doing more evil after the return.

6

JURISPRUDENCE

In law, as in theology, Mufid was the leading Imami scholar of his time. All the important jurists of the next generation were his students. His major work on jurisprudence is known as "The Convincing." It is an epitome of Imami law and served as a reference book for students and scholars. His student Tusi wrote a commentary on it and made it the basis of his Hadith collection entitled "The Refinement of Legal Decisions." This large work, recognized as the third canonical Imami collection, was begun during Mufid's lifetime.

Mufid also wrote on the principles of jurisprudence, that is, the principles according to which rules and regulations are found and derived from the revealed sources. A treatise by him on the subject survives in a short abridgment in the work of a later scholar, but his views are also found scattered in a number of his works and in written answers to questions sent to him by Imamis from other parts of the Muslim world. Mufid was instrumental in establishing and gaining acceptance for a role for reason in jurisprudence. His views became the basis on which later Imami jurists built.

His other works in the sphere of law consisted mainly of short polemical treatises on topics of dispute between Imamis and Sunnis, such as the legality of temporary marriage, which Imamis affirmed and other Muslims rejected, and the permissibility of washing of the shoes (instead of the feet) as part of the ritual ablutions before prayer, which Imamis rejected and Sunnis affirmed. He also wrote a work delineating all the differences in legal ordinances between Imamis and Sunnis. The interest of Imamis in such comparisons is noticeable for the Buyid period and reflects a desire on the part of the leadership to strengthen awareness of a distinct communal identity.

THE PRINCIPLES OF IMAMI JURISPRUDENCE

Traditionalist Imami Jurisprudence

In law, as in theology, in the period after the disappearance of the twelfth imam, Imamis continued at first to uphold the position that the Qur'an and Hadith were the only admissible sources. Their position continued to differ from the evolving Sunni position in two main respects. Firstly, whereas in Sunnism the only valid Hadith reports were from the Prophet, in Imamism all Hadith reports were from the imams and thought to have revealed status, whether or not they were traced back to the Prophet. This view of Hadith in Imamism was based on the belief that the religious knowledge of the imams was identical with the Prophet's, and that their pronouncements on the law always conformed to his practice or *Sunna*.

Secondly, in Sunnism, knowledge and study of the revealed texts was thought to confer upon the scholars the authority to rely on individual opinion and reasoning (*ijtihad*) for the purpose of deriving additional legal norms and for resolving new legal cases concerning which the revealed texts did not provide any clear guidance. In Imamism, however, scholars continued to assert, as they had done during the time of the imams, that the Prophetic revelation as expounded by the imams, and preserved in Hadith reports from them, contained comprehensive law and allowed for every eventuality. As before, Imami scholars would denounce the Sunni methods and rules of deriving the law as superfluous and leading to conjecture and arbitrariness, and they would insist that their own task as legal scholars was merely to find the rules and regulations laid down by the imams, not to derive new ones. They would cite the disagreements over rules and regulations that existed within the Sunni schools as proof of the falseness of *ijtihad* and of the spuriousness of Sunni traditions.

As we have seen in the last chapter, this traditionalism was reflected in the work of Kulini, known as "The Sufficient," and completed during the period of the "lesser occultation." But the work also shows that Imamis were already beginning to recognize the existence of, and to deal with, new theoretical problems arising from the absence of the imam. During the time of the imams Imamis could claim that their presence guarded the religious law against corruption and against the sort of disagreements that were rife in the Sunni schools. The main problem now, after the disappearance of the imam, was the existence within Imami Hadith of inconsistencies and divergences concerning the details of the law, which required not only justification (in view of earlier claims to being in possession of certain knowledge), but also that divergences be resolved by the scholars and without the possibility of appeal to the imam.

A number of reasons were given by Imamis for the existence of divergent Hadith reports. The two most common reasons, which were also cited by Kulini in a section devoted to the subject, were transmission by weak or unreliable transmitters, and the practice of dissimulation (*taqiyya*) by the imams. It was said that the imams sometimes chose to conceal their real views on questions of law or dogma because they knew that by revealing them they would be laying Imamis open to persecution by their Sunni enemies.

Kulini, as he himself indicates in the introduction to his work, envisaged his own collection as containing only authentic reports, and he implies that he has sifted through available Hadith by applying certain criteria. Imamis, he says, must refrain from using their own opinion when dealing with divergent Hadith reports and attempting to establish their authenticity. They must compare the reports with the Qur'an: those which agree with its statements are to be accepted as authentic, those which disagree are to be rejected. The other criteria he proposes for determining authenticity are the agreement of a report with the consensual position of Imamis and, rather unrealistically, its disagreement with the position of Sunnis. (As one would expect, these criteria are presented as having been stipulated by the imams themselves.)

Kulini's legal material, and the way it has been selected and arranged, shows that it had developed in the course of discussing and investigating the law, and along lines of thought not dissimilar to those followed by Sunni jurists. It also shows that, in terms of substance, the differences between Imami and Sunni law were (mostly) not greater than those that existed within Sunnism between one school of law and another. The main difference was that in a Sunni work of jurisprudence from the same period one finds, in addition to Hadith reports (mainly from the Prophet and his companions), opinions and arguments of earlier jurists and comments and additional regulations by the author, whereas in Kulini's work, descriptions of the law, as well as the reasoning behind its prescriptions, appear entirely in the form of Hadith from the imams.

Towards a More Rationalist Jurisprudence

After Kulini the idea that the law in its entirety can be expressed clearly through Hadith became increasingly difficult to maintain. There was a growing realization that total reliance on Hadith and traditionalist methods of Hadith criticism (such as those advocated by Kulini) was not sufficient for the purposes of systematizing Imami law or keeping pace with developments in the Sunni schools. Imamis needed to define their own position on questions arising from polemical exchanges with outsiders and from discussions within their own circles, and to provide supplementary regulations in areas of the law not dealt with fully or clearly in Hadith. Thus, they began to rely more and more on their own reasoning and interpretation of the revealed texts, much the same as their Sunni counterparts had been doing for a century or so but following somewhat different methods. And beginning with Mufid, Imami scholars began to establish and develop the principles on the basis of which they as jurists were authorized to expound the law. This too had begun much earlier in Sunnism, where large works detailing the norms of the law often included discussion and defense of the "principles of jurisprudence" (usul al-fiqh), and where, from the early fourth/tenth century, there began to appear works devoted entirely to study of those "principles."

Two different attempts to expound Imami law, based on different methods, are attested in the period after Kulini. Ibn al-Junayd al-Iskafi (d. 381/991) adopted the method of reasoning by analogy (qiyas), which was common in the Sunni schools and had come to be regarded as one of the four "roots" of Sunni jurisprudence, the others being the Qur'an, the Sunna of the Prophet (as preserved in Hadith), and the consensus of the scholars. Qiyas, as defined by Sunni jurists, was a restricted form of reasoning and to be applied only to the Qur'an and Hadith. It had replaced the use of personal opinion (ra'y) which was common among early jurists and judges. As Mufid later indicated, Ibn al-Junayd's works failed to gain acceptance among fellow Imamis because he had used the methods of Sunnis.

The other scholar was Ibn Babuya. Although his work, like Kulini's, was essentially a Hadith collection, and was subsequently recognized as the second of four canonical books of Imami Hadith, there was a significant difference between the two. In addition to the Hadith reports, Ibn Babuya's contained his own Qur'anic citations, summaries, comments, and additional regulations, in other words, his own (undisguised) contribution as a jurist.

Mufid's Principles of Jurisprudence

In Mufid's view there were serious faults with the jurisprudence of both Ibn al-Junayd and Ibn Babuya. Both relied on "weak" reports from single and/or unreliable transmitters. (Presumably Mufid had similar reservations about Kulini's inclusion of single-authority reports. But evidence for this is lacking. At one point he calls Kulini's collection one of the most important and useful works of the Shi'a.) Ibn Babuya failed to tackle adequately the problem of inconsistencies and disagreements in Hadith. And Ibn al-Junayd relied on inadmissible sources and methods: he used his own opinion and derived additional regulations from the Qur'an and Hadith by means of analogical reasoning.

The Problem of Divergence in Hadith. The "reliable" method that Mufid recommends for establishing the authenticity of reports from the imams is to be pursued only by experts in the religious sciences, not by ordinary Muslims. It consists of applying to the reports a number of criteria. In addition to "agreement with the Qur'an" and "agreement with the consensus of the Imami party," both of which are already attested for Kulini, Mufid asserted the principle of "wide attestation" or "multiple witnesses." But a more significant contribution was to argue in favor of a role for reason in the critical evaluation of Hadith reports, that is, in determining whether or not they are authentic and what their correct interpretation is.

Earlier scholars had cited dissimulation (*taqiyya*) as one of the reasons for the existence of contradictions and inconsistencies. But they (or the Hadith reports they adduced on this subject) had not proposed ways of ascertaining which reports originated by way of dissimulation. Imamis were often criticized for this by opponents who objected that if their imams had really allowed themselves to issue judgments and voice views on the basis of *taqiyya*, then how were their followers to distinguish truth from falsehood. Mufid took up the problem and argued that there were always scholars among the disciples of the imams who knew about the circumstances in which such reports had originated. Moreover, according to Mufid, one finds that reports based on *taqiyya* are never as widely attested as the reports conveying the real views of the imams. The "real" reports always correspond to the practice of the Imami party. The consensus of Imamis regarding any practice can never be based on statements uttered under conditions of *taqiyya* or falsely ascribed to the imams, but only on authentic statements by them transmitted through reliable witnesses and channels.

The Role of Consensus (*Ijma'*). The concept of consensus as a principle in jurisprudence was recognized in Sunni Islam and among the Mu'tazila. There it was envisaged as including the whole community (or, rather, the whole community as represented by its jurists). Moreover, it was regarded as an independent (though a minor) source of doctrine, alongside the Qur'an and Hadith. Thus, if the whole community was known to have agreed on a practice or an article of dogma not attested in the revealed sources, this agreement in itself constituted a valid and infallible source. Early Imamis, by contrast, denied the validity of consensus and any need for it, as their infallible imams offered certainty in all religious matters. They rejected the Sunni idea that "the whole community can never agree on an error." However, when the line of imams came to an end and Imamis began to deal with the problem of divergence in Hadith, the concept of consensus came in handy. But it was the consensus of the Imamiyya, not of the whole community, that Imamis appealed to. Furthermore, they envisaged this consensus as a means of resolving divergent reports, and not, as in Sunnism, as an additional source of doctrine.

Mufid's position on the role of consensus remained largely the same as that of his predecessors. One difference was that he was willing to accept the consensus of the whole Muslim community as a valid argument, provided, however, that it incorporated the opinion of the imam. This was more a polemical stance than real acceptance of a Sunni position. Imamis were often under attack for violating the consensus of the community on a number of legal and dogmatic issues. Against that, Mufid wanted to show that the Sunni concept of consensus was meaningless: in principle, it should include the views of jurists from the Family of the Prophet, that is, the imams and other 'Alid jurists, but in practice the Sunni jurists were known to have differed from 'Ali in many of their judgments and were opposed to his descendants. The Sunnis, in other words, have always contravened their own principle.

Still, Mufid did occasionally appeal to the consensus of Muslims as an additional argument, and he regarded it as sufficient proof of authenticity of isolated Hadith reports from the imams. This represented a small but significant change of attitude on the part of Imamis towards the Sunni tradition. It may be recalled that Kulini had advocated opposition to the view of Sunnis as one of the criteria for deciding between contradictory reports.

Against Reasoning by Analogy (Qiyas). Regarding analogical reasoning (*qiyas*), Mufid upheld the Imami position that it was not a sound procedure in jurisprudence. He denounced its use for deriving additional regulations as well as in Hadith criticism. When dealing with doubtful or contradictory Hadith reports, Imamis must use only rational proofs (*'aql*) and avoid analogical reasoning. One of the common Imami arguments against *qiyas* was that much of the law, concerning which there are clear statements in the Qur'an and Hadith, is lacking in analogy, which proves that the intentions of the Law Giver can never be discovered through such means. Besides, Imamis had no need for any of the rules or methods of deriving the law, since they had the statements of the imams to guide them.

Reason (*'aql*) as a Source. Mufid insisted that the guidance of the imams extended to all new cases or situations not covered by any specific ruling in the Qur'an or Hadith from the Prophet: for every new case that arises there is a clear stipulation from the imams, which the jurist must find and base his decision on. However, there appears to have been some development in Mufid's attitude to the problem of "new cases." In another work of his, where he describes a discussion he had with an opponent about the occultation, he admits the possibility that new cases can arise during the occultation, for which clear statements from the Prophet and the imams may be lacking. He says that in the very rare event that no statement is found, the jurist would know that the matter is up to the judgment of reason (*'aql*), for if God had wished to impose a judgment of revelation in that matter, He would have done that.

He gives the following as an example of a judgment based on reason: "If a person takes something by force from another person, he must return the thing itself if it still exists. If it doesn't, he must compensate for it with its like or, if its like does not exist, he must satisfy his adversary with that which removes the injustice. If he is unable or unwilling to do that, he will be answerable for it until the Day of Resurrection." This, effectively, was *ijtihad*, but Mufid does not call it that. The rejection of *ijtihad* (and equating it with personal opinion and analogical reasoning) was still part of the polemical definition of Imamism and remained so throughout the Buyid period. It is clear, though, that he regarded the Imami use of judgments based on reason as comparable in function to the Sunni practice of *ijtihad*, namely, to reach a legal opinion on matters not clearly stipulated in the revealed sources. He says that it is permitted to Imamis only when necessary, that is, when the imam is absent and his opinion cannot be sought, just as in Sunnism resort to *ijtihad* is permitted only in the absence of the Prophet.

Thus, with Mufid, Imami jurisprudence began to move away from the strict traditionalism of its formative period and towards a position more open to the use of reason. In developing his views on the methods and principles of jurisprudence, Mufid was concerned to establish a distinctive Imami position and, at the same time, to maintain the principle of certitude, which in early Imamism had been such an important part of its challenge to the Sunni schools of law. Thus, he rejected not only *ijtihad* and *qiyas* but also the single-authority Hadith reports, or rather, he restricted severely the validity of those reports by making their acceptance dependent on agreement with the Qur'an, reason, or consensus. And he admitted the use of reason as a tool in the understanding and interpretation of Hadith reports and as a minor source. Similar concerns characterized the legal thought of his successors among the scholars of the Buyid period, who built on his ideas. It was only much later, in the seventh/thirteenth century, that Imami jurists began to admit that they often worked on the basis of probability rather than certainty, and were practising *ijtihad*.

THE JURIST AS DEPUTY OF THE IMAM

With Mufid, we witness the beginning of a process whereby the Imami jurists were not only making greater and more explicit claims to religious authority than their traditionalist predecessors. They were also beginning to argue that some of the other functions of the imams have been delegated to them. They did this through discussing those areas of the law which dealt with the rights and functions of the imam as ruler and which corresponded to the functions of the imam/caliph in Sunni Islam as a secular ruler. These consisted of executing legal decisions and imposing the legal penalties stipulated in the Qur'an, leading the Holy War, leading the Friday prayer, and receiving and distributing the religious taxes.

The interest of Imami jurists in those aspects of the law was not purely academic. It reflected their growing involvement in the social and administrative affairs of their community and the need to legitimize that involvement. Centuries later, this process culminated in the claim of jurists to be, collectively, the general deputy of the hidden imam, with authority to control or even replace the existing government. The idea received its fullest articulation at the hands of Khomeini (d. 1989) who held that the person most suited to govern was the leading jurist. Back in the days of Mufid, however, jurists, though claiming to be the deputies of the imam in a number of his functions, continued to advocate non-involvement in politics.

Living under Illegitimate Government

The onset of the occultation did not bring about significant change in the Imami position on the status of existing government or how to interact with it. As Hadith and other sources indicate, Imamis continued to assert that the only just and legitimate ruler was the imam. And as before, they held that without the express permission of the imam it was forbidden to rise against an illegitimate and tyrannical ruler. This was seen as the task of the Mahdi who, upon his reappearance, would claim his rightful position with the sword. This contradiction in the Imami attitude to government was justified partly on the basis that unlawful rebellion would be dangerous and even destructive for the community, and partly on the basis that government was necessary for the implementation of the revealed law and, hence, that any government was better than no government.

Imamis were thus expected to accommodate themselves to the reality of living under illegitimate rule. Sometimes this involved cooperation with government. In fact, throughout the early development of Imamism leading Imamis were known to have cooperated with government and held office under it. A number of reports from the imams, dealing with various problems and concerns arising from the situation of life under illegitimate rule, are found in the early Hadith collections. The questions they address include whether or in what circumstances obedience to government was necessary, the validity of paying taxes to it and fighting on its behalf, whether it was permissible to do business with it and to accept office under it, and the validity of performing the Friday prayer in the rulers' mosques.

But the pronouncements of the imams on these questions, as found in Hadith, were not always uniform or sufficiently detailed. For example, some reports are categorical in their condemnation of working for government, while others permit it under certain conditions such as the ability of the holder of office to benefit the imam or his co-religionists. Thus, the scholars of the Buyid period began to respond to the needs of their community for clearer guidelines and rules (and, in the case of some scholars, to justify their own involvement with government) by treating those areas of the law in a more systematic manner.

According to Mufid, a believer is permitted, and sometimes obliged, to help the unjust in doing what is right. He is also permitted to work for them, to gain from them, and to make use of their wealth, provided it does not harm his fellow believers or involve him in acts of disobedience to the law. As for the wealth in the hands of rulers that has come to them specifically from the believers, if it is known to be that, then a believer may not accept any of it willingly. As for taking up office on their behalf, it is allowed only with the permission of the imam of the time and according to the conditions that he lays down. Although Mufid does not address the problem arising from the fact that the imam of the time was unavailable, this does not necessarily mean that he regarded taking up office with government during the occultation as illicit. As we have seen earlier, in his view the jurist was authorized to resolve "new cases" that arise during the absence of the imam. His position, therefore, might have been that before accepting office a believer must first seek the advice of the jurist who knows the conditions laid down by the imam and would be able to give the believer an opinion on its legality.

Judicial Authority in the Absence of the Imam

In the early fourth/tenth century it was widely accepted that judicial authority had been conferred upon the scholars by the imams. According to Hadith, the imams had instructed their followers not to seek judgment from the "judges of tyranny," that is, from non-Imamis appointed by the illegitimate Sunni government, and, instead, to submit their disputes to Imamis, who were pious and knowledgeable in the Hadith and precepts of the imams, and to accept their judgments. The imams are reported to have said that accepting the decision of a "judge of tyranny" and rejecting that of an Imami scholar amounted to unbelief.

In the Buyid period it became possible for the first time to administer Imami law. But since judges, witnesses, and other legal officials were appointed by, or took up their positions on behalf of, the illegitimate rulers, this naturally presented Imamis with a dilemma. Mufid attempted to resolve it on the basis that the acts and judgments of those appointed would be valid not because of their official appointment but by virtue of the imam having delegated his authority to jurists. He tells us that authentic Hadith reports confirm that the imams have delegated to the jurists of their Shi'a all the functions of judges. These jurists and those of them who have been appointed as judges by the tyrannical ruler must judge only in accordance with Imami law. However, under conditions of *taqiyya* due to fear for one's life or religion, if the jurists are compelled to, they may judge according to Sunni law, provided that decisions made under *taqiyya* do not cause the shedding of innocent blood. This, more or less, remained the Imami position under Mufid's successors.

Execution of Prescribed Penalties

Imamis, like other Muslims, tended to assign to the imam the sole right to execute, or to authorize the execution of, the penalties prescribed by the *shari'a* for certain major offences. These penalties are known as the *hudud*. They include flogging for adultery, hand amputation for theft, and killing for blasphemy.

On the basis of Hadith sources, it would seem that the common view of Imamis in the early fourth/tenth century was that

individual Imamis needed authorization by the imam to execute these penalties. Some held that in a few cases, such as in the
case of punishment for adultery, an individual who knows the
law may deal with the situation himself and without reference
to the imam.

Mufid, followed by other scholars of the Buyid period, went
much further. He affirmed that the imams had delegated this
function to the jurists. The latter were permitted to carry out
the prescribed punishments on their own children and slaves,
as well as on "those of their people whom they were in charge
of." Moreover, an Imami appointed by the existing ruler to execute the legal punishments was obliged to do so in accordance
with Imami law. Other Imamis were obliged to help him in his
endeavors, provided that in obeying the ruler he has not relin-
quished any element of his faith or disobeyed God.

Leading Holy War (Jihad)

Muslim jurists distinguished between two kinds of *jihad*: *jihad*
for defensive purposes and *jihad* for the spread of Islam and its
territories. According to the Sunni jurists, the imam had a main
role in organizing wars of *jihad* and it was the duty of Muslims
to participate in them, regardless of whether he was sinful.
Sunnis also tended to sanction campaigns in enemy territory or
on the borders, undertaken by individuals and groups on their
own initiative and in the absence of an imam.

According to early Imamis, *jihad* for the spread of Islam
may only be undertaken in the presence of a legitimate imam
and under his leadership or that of his representative. Mufid,
however, held that an Imami official appointed by the illegitimate ruler had the duty to conduct (offensive) *jihad* against
unbelievers, and even against some Muslim grave sinners, and
that it was the duty of his fellow Imamis to assist him. It is not

clear on what basis Mufid justified his view. It is also not clear whether his aim was to accord legitimacy to existing practices. Other scholars of the Buyid period did not uphold his doctrine. Tusi, the last of those scholars, held that in the absence of the imam, *jihad* against the enemies of Islam was suspended and only defensive *jihad* might be carried out. According to him, guarding the frontiers of Islam was a praiseworthy act, irrespective of whether or not an imam was present. (There is no evidence that he regarded the scholars as responsible for organizing defensive *jihad* or calling upon the people to wage it.) It was Tusi's views, not Mufid's, that influenced Imami juristic thought on the subject for several centuries to come.

Leading Friday Prayer

The congregational Friday prayer service takes the place of the daily midday prayer. It is performed in the central mosque of a town and includes as its main feature a sermon. The convening of the service (as well as of religious festival services) was regarded by early Muslims as the duty of the ruler or his appointed deputy, who might be a governor or a judge. Its observance symbolized one's loyalty to Islam and allegiance to its guardian, the head of the community.

Evidence from the historical sources suggests that early Imamis and other Shi'is, who did not recognize the caliph as a legitimate ruler, would not join other Muslims for the perform-ance of this duty. However, it is not clear whether Imamis conducted their own congregational Friday services or, if they did, whether they stopped convening them (and regarded the duty as having lapsed) when the twelfth imam disappeared. Early Hadith reports suggest that they regarded attendance at Friday services as obligatory, but also that in certain circum-stances it was permissible to perform the prayers by oneself or in a group without a prayer leader, or even with Sunnis out of dissimulation. However, as modern scholars have often observed, Hadith is not necessarily an accurate reflection of existing practice.

In the Buyid period, when Imamis were encouraged to celebrate their festivals and to perform their rituals openly, it became important to regulate the observance of congregational prayers. Mufid argued that the imams had delegated their authority to the qualified jurists. The latter had the right to assemble their fellow Imamis for all the congregational prayers, provided they could do so without incurring "shameful behavior on the part of the evil people" (a probable reference to the attacks that Imamis sometimes suffered at the hands of Sunni mobs when celebrating their festivals).

Similar views were expressed by Mufid's pupil Tusi. But the question of legality of the Friday service in the absence of the imam was already a controversial issue in Tusi's time and remained so among later scholars. The dominant tendency to regard it as prohibited during the occultation may be related to the fact that in the minds of Imamis its observance was closely associated with Sunni Islam.

Collection and Distribution of Religious Taxes

Two kinds of taxes were regarded by early Muslims as ritual duties: the alms or poor tax (*zakat*) and the tax known as the fifth (*khums*). Both taxes are mentioned in the Qur'an. But whereas the Sunnis interpreted the Qur'anic statement on *khums* as a reference to tax payable on moveable booty taken in holy war, the Imamis took it to be a reference to tax payable on several items, including booty, minerals, and profits from trade and agriculture. The other main difference was that whereas in Sunnism these taxes were payable to the existing ruler, in

Imamism they were held to be payable to the imams, who had the sole right in their collection and distribution. Both held that it is sometimes possible for the individual to pay the *zakat* directly to its recipients, namely, orphans, the poor, those in debt, and needy travelers.

In the case of revenues from the *khums*, according to Imami law the imams were entitled to half of them and the other half went to the poor, orphans, and needy travelers from among the Prophet's descendants, who, on account of their holy status, were not entitled to alms. (Because almsgiving was regarded as an act of purification, alms were believed to consist of the "defilements" of people.) In addition to their own share of the *khums*, the imams had the right to keep any excess, but they were also responsible for making up any shortages. And there were no rules as to what they might spend their share of the *khums* on.

The sources speak of agents who collected the revenues from these taxes and delivered them regularly to the imams. They also suggest that this went on during the period of the "lesser occultation," when the twelfth imam was supposed to be in touch with his followers and in control of the network of agents. They do not mention scholars or jurists as having any role to play in those operations.

Things changed in the Buyid period when the Imami jurists were able to control some of these tax payments within their own community. Mufid claimed a main role for them in the control of *zakat* payments. He stated that in the absence of the imam or his representative it is the duty of people to carry the payments to the trustworthy jurists who would then transfer them to their recipients, the jurists being more knowledgeable than others about who the right recipients were. From his remarks, and from those of his successors, it would seem that in this area of the law the early jurists regarded themselves as representatives not of the imam but of the donor of *zakat*.

In one respect, however, Mufid's views did not find general acceptance among Buyid and other later scholars: whereas he regarded it *incumbent* on the believers to deliver the *zakat* to jurists, the other scholars regarded the individual believer as responsible himself for its distribution and said it was *permissible* to deliver it to trustworthy Imamis, preferably, to jurists.

But it was the *khums* that was the main source of revenue for Imami leaders who used it to manage the affairs of their community and to finance Imami learning. As in the case of *zakat*, discussion of the incumbency of *khums* and its management during the absence of the imam first appears in the writings of Mufid. He tells us that there were marked differences between Imamis as to what happens to the share of the imam during the occultation. Whereas some held that the duty lapses, others claimed that it was obligatory to bury the *khums* revenues and cited a Hadith report which said that "the earth will bring forth its treasures when the Mahdi appears." Another group said it was recommended that the revenues are distributed among the poor of the Shi'a.

But the view preferred by Mufid was that the donor should put aside the share of the imam as long as he (the donor) is alive, and when death approaches he should appoint a trustworthy Imami as guardian over the goods, and so on until the imam appears and the goods may be delivered to him. The justification given by Mufid for this view is, firstly, that the payment of *khums* like that of *zakat* does not lapse in the absence of a rightful recipient and, secondly, that it is not right to dispose of a person's property without his consent. He appears to have later changed his mind about what to do with the imam's share during his absence: he said it should be given to the poor, orphans, and wayfarers from among the descendants of the Prophet. And although he did not indicate who should undertake its distribution (or the distribution of the share of the Prophet's Family), given his views regarding the management of *zakat*, it is not unlikely that he had the jurists in mind.

As in the case of *zakat*, Mufid's successors did not assign a main or exclusive role to the jurists in the distribution of the *khums* and preferred, instead, to speak of trustworthy Imamis (who might, of course, often be jurists). It was about three centuries later that jurists began again to claim, as Mufid had once done, that the religious taxes must be administered by themselves. But by then the general tendency among them was to recognize themselves as deputies of the imam for the collection and distribution of those taxes, whereas the earlier jurists had regarded themselves (as well as other "trustworthy Imamis") as deputies of the donor.

RITUAL PRACTICES AND LAWS SPECIFIC TO IMAMISM: EMBLEMS OF COMMUNAL IDENTITY

We have said above that by the early fourth/tenth century it was already clear that in matters of law and ritual most of the differences between Imamism and Sunnism were not greater than those that existed between one Sunni school of law and another. Minor differences were found in various aspects of the five-times daily prayer ritual and in the fast of the month of Ramadan. For example, the Imami call to prayer included the additional statement "Hasten to the best of work."

But there were also significant differences with Sunnism, which Imamis tended to emphasize as marks of their separate identity. Some were found in the laws of inheritance and of divorce, with Imami law being more accommodating towards women than Sunni law. For example, in the Sunni law of inheritance, relatives through a male link are given preference, whereas Imami law does not differentiate between relatives through male links and relatives through female links. This characteristic of Imami law has been attributed to the status that Fatima, the Prophet's daughter and 'Ali's wife, occupied in Imamism and the fact that the imams, her descendants, were regarded as heirs of the Prophet. However, the desire to diverge from some of the practices of the larger Muslim community was probably more relevant in the evolution of those special features of Imami law.

Another well-known difference was in the law of "temporary marriage" known as *mut'a* (lit., enjoyment). This is marriage for a fixed term and involving a predetermined financial arrangement whereby the woman receives a fixed sum. Imamis believed that it was sanctioned by the Qur'an (Q. 4: 24) "When you have had your enjoyment of them then give them their reward as a duty." However, the meaning and the legal status of the verse in question were disputed, and the practice was specifically forbidden among Sunnis or, rather, had come to be by the third/ninth century.

Those differences were the subject of frequent polemical exchanges between Imamis and Sunnis, which became more intense during the Buyid period when Imamis would have been more open about their laws and more outspoken in defending them. Mufid devoted many pages to rebutting the criticisms of opponents and defending the peculiarities of Imami law, a good amount of which is extant. As his writings indicate, the issues and the arguments used by both sides were not all new, but they were becoming more complex and nuanced, as more of the implications of the Imami positions were questioned and debated. The Sunnis, who had come to tolerate juridical divergence as a fact of life within the Sunni schools, continued to use against the Imamis the argument that by adopting those practices and legal doctrines the latter have introduced innovations and have deviated from the consensus of the Muslim community. In defending those practices Mufid sought to prove that Imami law was the only correct interpretation of the revealed law.

Mufid on Temporary Marriage (Mut'a)

Mufid is reported to have written three treatises on the question of temporary marriage and he defended the practice in a work written in response to questions sent to him from the district of Khurasan in eastern Iran. The importance that he (and several other Imamis, both before and after him) attached to tackling this subject is unlikely to have been due to practical considerations such as widespread practice among Imamis. It may rather be related to the fact that this was an area of the law where traditional evidence found in Sunni sources tended to support the Imami position and to undermine the Sunni. On the basis of that evidence Imamis could point out that some of the early Sunni authorities had allowed the practice and had transmitted reports indicating that it was common during the time of the Prophet, and that it was the second caliph 'Umar who prohibited it and contravened thereby what the Qur'an and the Prophet had allowed.

Visiting the Shrines of the Imams (Ziyara)

Another specifically Imami practice and perhaps one of the most important expressions of a separate communal identity was the ritual of *ziyara* or visitation to the shrines of the imams. The practice appears to have first developed in connection with Husayn, 'Ali's son, who was later recognized as the third Imami imam, and not long after his martyrdom in 61/680 at the battle of Karbala' in southern Iraq, at the hands of the hated Umayyads. There is also evidence that in the third/ninth century Husayn's grave was visited frequently as a place of Shi'i pilgrimage. In 236/850 it was destroyed at the orders of the pro-Sunni caliph Mutawakkil, as part of his attempt to stop the practice. In the Buyid period 'Ali's grave in Najaf, which had only recently been "discovered," became established as the definite site of his burial and, like Husayn's, frequently visited. The shrines of the other imams (located in Baghdad and Samarra in Iraq, Medina in Arabia, and Mashhad in Iran) were also gaining importance as regular places of visitation.

The growing importance of those visitations was reflected in the special attention that the Buyid rulers paid to the shrines of the imams, taking measures to protect them and spending money on their restoration and adornment. That was also the time when the elaborate rituals for their performance were drawn up and formalized and a genre of literature referred to as "books of *ziyarat*" emerged. The books served as guides and instruction manuals and were probably intended for use by scholars to instruct ordinary Imamis in the proper rites of *ziyara*. One of the earliest known is by Mufid's teacher Ibn Quluya, which Mufid relied on in the composition of a work of his own on the subject.

Mufid's work consists of detailed descriptions of the supplications that the believer pronounces before going on those pilgrimages, the rites and rituals that he performs and participates in, and the formulaic expressions that he pronounces at each step of the ritual. It also includes traditional information about the benefits a believer receives and the rewards he merits by making a *ziyara*, by making it on certain holy days, and by performing certain rituals. The rewards from a *ziyara* to 'Ali or to Husayn were said to far exceed those from the *hajj* (the annual pilgrimage to Mecca, which is obligatory on every physically able Muslim at least once in a lifetime, provided he has the means to undertake it). According to one report, performing a *ziyara* to Husayn's shrine in Karbala is "more meritorious than twenty pilgrimages to Mecca."

7

CONCLUSION

As we have seen, Mufid's particular importance was in his admission and defense of a role for human reasoning in religion, which he combined with an insistence on the status of the revealed sources as the basis of all Imami doctrine. With him the role of the Imami scholar began to develop beyond that of transmitter and clarifier of the imams' teachings. Whereas earlier scholars had tended to present their polemical and theological reasoning as derived from, or implicit in, the Hadith of the imams, Mufid helped establish the idea that the scholar was authorized to construct independent rational arguments and to use them in support of the historical claims, beliefs, and practices of the Imamiyya. This was one step away from acceptance of the essentially Mu'tazili idea that all the fundamentals of religion are to be established entirely by the application of reason to the revelation, which took place at the hands of Mufid's successors and remained characteristic of the dominant current in Imamism throughout its history.

As regards the content of Imami theology, we have seen that the picture of Mufid as instrumental in the introduction of Mu'tazili concepts and in its transformation from a determinist to an anti-determinist stance is no longer tenable, and that development along those lines had already begun in Imamism in the latter part of the third/ninth century. His contribution was nevertheless significant. He formulated new rational arguments and solutions to problems arising from the inconsistencies and ambiguities of the Hadith sources and from objections voiced by opponents, as we have seen, for example, in his treatment of the doctrines of *bada'* and *raj'a*. He also broke new ground in his use of Mu'tazili principles, namely, the principles of "best interests" and "commanding only that which is possible," as the basis of arguments on the necessity of the imamate and the occultation.

Mufid's influence on later Imami theology remained, however, limited. Whereas his theology had been close to that of the Mu'tazili school of Baghdad, his student Murtada, who was the leading theologian of the next generation, adopted much from the doctrine of the Mu'tazili school of Basra and, thus, came to differ from Mufid on many questions of detail. It was Murtada's views, and not Mufid's, that were to be upheld by later Imami theologians and to have a lasting influence. On the other hand, one must not exaggerate the importance of those differences between Mufid and the later theologians, as they had no bearing on the fundamental belief in the imamate and its role in salvation. Mufid's successors continued to uphold the role of the imam as intercessor for his community and to reject the Mu'tazili doctrine of the unconditional and permanent punishment of the sinner. Moreover, the rational arguments he had formulated in support of the imamate and the occultation became the framework for all later works on the subject.

Also influential were Mufid's attempts to prove the validity of the Imami imamate and to discredit its opponents by arguments based on the mainstream historical tradition and Imami traditional sources. His *Book of Guidance*, the most important of the works he wrote for that purpose, became a reference for later Hadith scholars and a source used by preachers.

In the field of jurisprudence Mufid was the first Imami scholar to speak of reason as an admissible source and as an interpretative tool in Hadith criticism. In developing his views on the use of reason and other principles of jurisprudence Mufid established the basis of a distinctive Imami position, which his successors built on and which on a number of points remained part of the Imami jurisprudential tradition. In one respect, however, Mufid's views on the role of reason in law proved premature. He had recognized the possibility that new cases may occasionally arise during the occultation, for which clear statements from the imams do not exist, and had argued that such cases may be resolved independently by the qualified scholar. But his pupil Tusi did not recognize the validity of rational legal knowledge that is independent of the revealed texts and continued to insist that for every new case that arises there is a statement from the imams. Moreover, Mufid's position on the status of single-authority reports – that on their own they do not give rise to certain knowledge – was effectively reversed by Tusi who asserted that their use was admissible, on the basis that they had been generally accepted by the Imami community during the time of the imams. Tusi's views were to gain wide (and uncritical) acceptance among Imami jurists down to the seventh/thirteenth century.

Finally, we have seen that Mufid was an important contributor to the process whereby the Imami jurists were beginning to legitimize their growing involvement in the affairs of their community by arguing that some of the functions of the hidden imam have devolved on them. It is true that on a number of issues (for example, the legality of conducting offensive *jihad* during the absence of the imam and whether the religious taxes were to be administered solely by the jurists) Mufid's views failed to gain acceptance and over the next three centuries some of the more moderate views came to prevail. But it was

Mufid who began to treat those areas of the law in a systematic manner and with creative interpretation and, thus, opened the way for the developments which have continued until recent times and in which the scholars have been able to claim one after another of the functions of the imam.

FURTHER READING

A certain amount of scholarship on Mufid already exists in European languages, none of it for the general reader. I have benefited particularly from the studies and insights of two scholars who have dealt with the theology of Mufid in some depth: Martin J. McDermott (*The Theology of al-Shaikh al-Mufid*, Beirut, 1978) and Paul Sander (*Zwischen Charisma und Ratio*, Berlin, 1994). McDermott's book is well known both in the West and in the Islamic world where it has been translated into Arabic and Persian. The more recent work of Sander is in German and much less known in the field than that of McDermott. Sander's findings serve as a corrective to the widely held view that Imami dogma underwent radical change at the hands of Mufid. My references in Chapter 5 to a recent reassessment of Mufid's role in the development of Imami theology are to his work.

For the best outline of the general development of Imami theology, which includes discussion of Mufid's role, see the readable article by Wilferd Madelung, "Imamism and Mu'tazilite Theology," in T. Fahd (ed.), *Le Shi'isme imamite* (Colloque de Strasbourg 1968, Paris, 1970).

The most important of Mufid's extant theological treatises is his *Awa'il al-maqalat* (Principal theses). It has been translated into French by Dominique Sourdel and appeared together with a long introduction as "L'Imamisme vu par le Cheikh al-Mufid" in *Revue des Etudes Islamiques* 40 (1972).

There is no single work on Mufid as a jurist in a European language. Aspects of his juristic thought have been discussed by McDermott (Chapter XI, "Legal matters") and in almost every work that deals with the early development of this branch of Imami learning. Most of these works are inaccessibly written. For a good summary of the history of Imami law, which includes a discussion of

Mufid and other Buyid scholars, see Hossein Modarressi, *An Introduction to Shi'i Law: a Bibliographical Study* (London, 1984). The article by W. Madelung, "Authority in Twelver Shi'ism in the Absence of the Imam" in G. Makdisi, D. Sourdel, and J. Sourdel-Thomine (eds.), *La notion d'autorité au Moyen Age: Islam, Byzance, Occident* (Paris, 1982) is a concise and clear treatment of the early Imami conception of the sources of legal authority and the role of the Buyid scholars (including Mufid) in its development.

Mufid's *Kitab al-Irshad* (Book of Guidance), on which is based much of my discussion of his historical treatment of the imamate, has been translated into English by I. K. A. Howard as *The Book of Guidance into the Lives of the Twelve Imams* (London, 1981). There is also a translation into French of his work on the battle of the Camel: M. Rouhani (trans.), *La victoire de Bassora ou al-Jamal, par Cheikh al Moufid* (Paris, 1974).

For Shi'ism in general, two of the best introductory works are Moojan Momen, *An Introduction to Shi'i Islam* (Oxford, 1985), and Heinz Halm, *Shi'ism* (Edinburgh, 1991).

INDEX

'Abbasid dynasty 6, 18, 27, 47, 49
'Abd al-Jabbar 22–3, 28
Abu Ahmad al-Musawi 21
Abu al-Faraj Isfahani 49
Abu al-Hasan al-Ash'ari 23, 90
Abu al-Jaysh al-Muzaffar al-Balkhi 28
Abu Bakr 36
Abu Ja'far Muhammad al-Tusi *see* Tusi
Abu Ja'far Muhammad ibn Babuya
      al-Qummi *see* Ibn Babuya
'Adud al-Dawla 19, 28
adultery 125
Age of Ignorance 57
Agha Khan 3
Akhu Muhsin 27
'Ali, caliph/imam
  as designated by the Prophet 35–6
    Hadith reports on 38–43
  Hanbali recognition of 24
  as infallible 43–6
  knowledge,
    of the future, his own murder 62
    of the law 42–3
  miraculous incident of *jinn* 67–8
  as most excellent of Prophet's
    companions 35–8
  Qur'an collection/codex of 64–6
  as successor to the Prophet, Sunni
    and Shi'i views compared 1–3
  the visiting of his grave 133
'Alids ('Ali's descendants)
  Buyids in Baghdad and 20–1
  support among scholars for 6
  Zaydi view of eligibility of 2
  as Family of the Prophet 4
almsgiving 128

anthropomorphism 86, 91, 98
'aql (reason) 119
Ash'aris, Ash'ari theology 23, 90, 91
'Ashura' festival 20
attributes, divine, Mu'tazili doctrine of
    86, 89
  rejection by Ash'aris 91
  rejection by early Imamis 99
  later Imami views 100–1

bada' (change of divine decree) 101–2
Baghdad 11
  Buyid governance 18–21
  as main center of Imamism 17
  Mu'tazili theologians in 22–3
  execution of Hallaj and Shalmaghani
    72
  Mufid's life in 27–30
Baghdadian Mu'tazila 22, 136
al-Baqir, Muhammad 5
Baqillani 23, 28
barzakh (Purgatory) 108, 109
Basran Mu'tazila 22–3, 136
belief and unbelief *see* faith
believers and interaction with
    unjust/illegitimate
    government 121–3
best interests of man and God's acts
    78–9, 85, 88, 90, 103–5, 136
"Book of Guidance" *(Kitab al-Irshad)*
    35–6, 37, 136
"books of *ziyarat*" 133
Buyids 18–19
  cultural climate under 21–2
  Imamis under 19–21
  Isma'ilis and 25–7

Buyids (*cont.*):
　shrines of the imams and 133
　Sunnis under 23–5
　see also Zaydi Shi'ism
Byzantines 26

caliphate *see* imamate
Camel, Battle of 43–4
"commanding only that which is
　　possible to fulfil", principle of
　　58, 88, 103, 136
"commanding the right and forbidding
　　the wrong", principle of 88–9
companions of the Prophet 24, 25, 37–8
　First Civil War and 43–5
compensation, doctrine of 103–4
compulsion to disobedience,
　　determination as 99, 105–6
consensus *(ijma')* 62, 97, 115, 116,
　　117–18, 120, 132
"Convincing, The" 111

Dar al-'Ilm (House of Learning),
　　Baghdad 20
Day of Judgement 87, 108
Day of Resurrection 109–10
delegation
　to imams of the creation,
　　exaggerated doctrine 74
　to man of the power to act 99,
　　105–6
designation *(nass)* to imamate 2, 6, 31,
　　32, 34, 47, 50, 52, 67, 101
　of 'Ali 38–41
determination, God's, and human free
　　will/choice
　Ash'ari view 90
　early Imami view 105–6
　Ibn Babuya, foreknowledge and
　　pre-estimation debate 106
　Mufid's view
　　belief and unbelief 106–7
　　man's acts 105–6
　Mu'tazili view 88
dissimulation *(taqiyya)* 7, 113, 117,
　　124, 127

divorce laws 130–1

Egypt, Fatimid conquest of 27
evil present in the world 104–5
exaggeration *(ghuluww)* 9, 60, 70–5
extremism *see* exaggeration

faith and salvation
　definition of faith 107
　God's determination of belief and
　　unbelief 106–7
　works and
　　in Ash'arism 90–1
　　in Mu'tazilism 87–8
　　in early Imamism 107–8
　　in Mufid's theology 108–9
Family of the Prophet 4, 5, 27, 38,
　　50, 118, 130
Fatimids 25–7
Fitna (First Civil War) 43, 45
foreknowledge, pre-estimation and
　　106, *see* determination
four rightly guided caliphs 1–2, 34, 36
free choice/will and divine
　　determination/predestination
　　88, 90, 99, 105–7
Friday prayer 126–7

Ghadir Khumm
　tradition of 38–42
　festival of 20
ghayba see occultation
ghulat, ghuluww (exaggerators,
　　exaggeration) 9, 70–5
gnosticism 8–10, 70–2
God's acts and man's best interests
　　78–9, 85, 88, 90, 103–5, 136
government and Imami jurists 121–3

Hadith
　authenticity question and criticism
　　by Kulini 114, 115
　　by Mufid, in jurisprudence
　　116–17
　　by Mufid, in theology 96–8
　authority (or status) of 3–4, 32, 64

in early Imami theology 92–3
in traditionalist Imami
    jurisprudence 112–13
on change of divine decree (*bada'*)
    101
divergences in, pertaining to the law
    113–14, 116–17, 119, 122
on existence of the Mahdi 76–7
on free choice and divine
    determination 105–7
on Friday prayer 126–7
Imami, compared with Sunni Hadith
    3, 14–15, 114
on imams after death 68–9
on interaction with illegitimate
    government 122
on necessity of imamate as God's
    Proof on earth 57
on pre-existence of human soul
    72–3
Qur'an as word/speech of God and
    100–1
on seeking judgement from
    Imami scholars 123–4
use of reason and
    in theology 92, 93, 95
    in jurisprudence 116–7, 119
hajj (pilgrimage) 69–70, 133
Hakim (Fatimid caliph) 26, 27
Hallaj 72
Hanbalis 24–5
Hasan 39, 46
Hassan (poet) 41–2
Heaven (Paradise) 72, 104, 108
Hell 72, 91, 110
    Purgatory (*barzakh*) and 108, 109
heresy
    divergence and necessity of imamate
        6, 56–7
    exaggeration in Shi'ism as 8–9,
        70–5
    Imami literature on 14, 70–1
hidden imam *see* Mahdi
holy war 125–6
hudud (prescribed penalties) 124–5
Husayn 20, 39, 132–3

Ibn Babuya 15, 28, 29, 103
    attack on rationalist theology
        (*kalam*) 94
    debate on completeness of Qur'an
        65
    debate on God's will and man's acts
        106–7
    debate on infallibility of prophets
        59
    debate on nature of Qur'an 101
    defense of *bada'* 102
    defense of occultation 52
    Hadith collection as work of
        jurisprudence 116
Ibn al-Junayd al-Iskafi 115, 116
Ibn Quluya, Ja'far 28, 101, 102, 133
ijma' (consensus) 117–18
ijtihad (individual reasoning) 44,
    112–13, 120
ilham (divinely imparted knowledge,
    inspiration) 3, 7–8, 31, 61
imamate
    administrative functions of, in
        Imami jurisprudence
        delegation to Imami jurists
            121, 124, 125, 127, 128,
            129–30
        execution of prescribed penalties
            124–5
        imposing judicial decisions
            123–4
        leading holy war 125–6
        leading Friday Prayer 126–7
        taxes, collection of 128–30
    historical tradition and sectarian
        disputes over 1–2, 33–5
        'Ali's excellence 35–8
        'Ali's infallibility 43–5
        designation of 'Ali 38–42
        existence of twelfth imam 51–3
        Hasan and al-Rida's conduct
            46–7
        between Imamis and Zaydis
            47–51
    Imami concepts of 31–3
        adoption of Twelverism 12

imamate (*cont.*):
    depoliticized, as permanent
      religious office 6
    doctrine of occultation 10–12,
      51–3
    early doctrine 7–8, 107
    exaggeration/gnosticism,
      opposition to and influence by
      8–9, 70–5
    infallibility 58–60
    knowledge 60–3
    knowledge of additional
      Qur'anic revelations 64–5
    life after death 68–9
    miracles 67
    necessity and doctrinal
      uniformity 56–8
    as only legitimate government
      121–2
    pre-existence in World of
      Shadows 72–3
    role in salvation 8, 31, 107–9,
      136
    superhuman qualities 31–3
    rational arguments pertaining to
      Imami imamate 55–6
    debate on completeness of
      Qu'ran 65–7
    imams' knowledge 62–3
    imams after death 68–70
    infallibility 58–60
    miracles 67–8
    necessity theory 56–8
    twelfth imam, occultation of
      75–82
    unacceptable exaggeration and
      70–5
    "wide attestation" as criterion of
      authenticity of Hadith on 35,
      68, 97
Imami Shi'ism vii–viii, 2–3, *et passim*
    Buyid governance and 19–21
    early developments 4–12, 14–15
    Fatimid Isma'ili challenge to 26–7
    literature 13–14
    rivalry with Zaydis 47–8

    see also Ithna'ashariyya (Twelverism)
imams after death 68–70
imams' shrines, the visiting of 132–4
imams' pre-existence in World of
    Shadows 9, 72–5
Imposter 81
incorporeality of God, Mu'tazili
    doctrine 86
infallibility of imamate 7, 31–2, 43–5,
    57, 58–60, 77, 118
    Mufid and dispute over possibility of
      "small errors" 74–5
inheritance laws 130–1
inspiration, doctrine of imams' 3, 31,
    49, 61–2
intercession 69, 84, 87, 108
"intermediate rank" of sinner in
    Mu'tazili theology 87–8
Iraq
    Fatimid Isma'ili missionaries'
      presence in 26–7
    festivals in 19–20, 23–4
Islam and faith 107
Isma'il 101, 102
Isma'ili Shi'ism 2–3, 72
    Buyids' reign and 25–7
Ithna'ashariyya (Twelverism) 1, 12
    see also Imami Shi'ism

jihad, offensive and defensive 125–6
jinn, report of 'Ali's confrontation
    with, question of authenticity
    67–8
jurisprudence, (Imami)
    authority in absence of the imam
      121–30, 137–8
    distinctive ritual practices and laws,
      emphasis on 130–2
    emergent rationalism 15, 114–16
    execution of prescribed penalties
      124–5
    Friday prayer 126–7
    interaction with illegitimate
      government 121–3
    jihad 125–6
    judicial authority 123–4

jurists as deputy of hidden imam
121
Mufid's principles of 115
  against analogical reasoning 119
  consensus, role of 117–18
  criticism of Ibn al-Junayd and Ibn
    Babuya 116
  problem of divergence in Hadith
    116–17
  reason as a source 119–20, 137
  rejection of *ijtihad* 120
Mufid's position on
  devolved authority of hidden
    imam 137–8:
  judicial authority 124; execution
    of prescribed penalties 125;
    leading holy war 125–6;
    leading Friday prayer 127;
    collection of taxes 128–30
  interaction with illegitimate
    government 123
  temporary marriage (*mut'a*) 132
  visiting the shrines of the imams
    133
Mufid's works on 111–12
taxes, collection and distribution of
  127–30
traditionalist principles of 112–14
jurisprudence, (Sunni)
  principles of 115
  admissibility of *ijtihad* 112–3
  Hanbali opposition to rationalism in
    24
justice, Mu'tazili doctrine of 87–9
  Ash'ari theology 90
  Imami theological developments
    99, 103

Ka'ba rituals 69–70
al-Kafi 28, 95 *see* "The Sufficient"
kalam see theology
kasb (acquisition of responsibility)
  doctrine 90, 105
al-Kazim, Musa 6
Khomeini viii, 121
khums (fifth) tax 127–30

knowledge of the imams 3, 7–8,
  31–2, 42–3, 49, 60–3
al-Kulini, Muhammad ibn Ya'qub 14,
  17, 28, 96, 113–14, 115, 116,
  118

law of Islam *see shari'a*

madhhab (school of jurisprudence) 24
Mahdi (hidden or twelfth imam)
  'Alid rights and 2
  as avenger against tyranny 122
  as source of religious authority 3
  authority devolved on jurists 137–8
  doctrine of necessity of imamate and
    57
  doctrine of occultation 10–12,
    51–3, 75–6
    problem of new cases during
      119
    proof and purpose of existence
      76–9
    proof of identity 81–2
    reasons for non-appearance
      79–81
  messianism and 5
  Muhammad b. 'Abdallah and 48–9,
    50
Ma'mun 47, 86
man as spirit 108–9
mawla 38, 41–2
messianism 5, 70
miracles 67–8, 81–2
monotheism of Mu'tazilism 85–6, 91
"most excellent, the", doctrine of 50
  divergent views on 35–8
Mu'awiya 43–4, 46
Mufid, Shaykh
  education and career vii–viii,
    17–18, 21, 24, 27–30
  overview of 135–8
  Imami imamate, historical defense
    32–3
  "Book of Guidance" 35, 140
  'Ali as most excellent companion
    35–8

Mufid, Shaykh (cont.):
 'Ali's designation 38, 40–2
 'Ali's knowledge of law 42–3
 'Ali's infallibility and
  companions' errors 44–5
 'Ali al-Rida's relations with
  Ma'mun 47
 doctrine of "the most excellent"
  50
 doctrine of occultation 52–3
 Hasan's actions and 46
 rational arguments and 55–6
 jurisprudence, his position on
  divergence in Hadith 116–17
  execution of prescribed penalties
   125
  Friday prayer 127
  interaction between believer and
   the unjust 121, 124
  jihad 125–6
  reason as a source 119–20
  reasoning by analogy 119
  role of consensus 118
  taxes, collection of 128–30
  temporary marriage 132
  visiting the shrines of the imams
   133
  works on 111–12
 theology,
  'Alid codex and 65–7
  belief and unbelief 106–7
  centrality of imamate doctrine in
   83–4
  doctrine of bada' 102
  "finer matters of theology" 95
  God's acts and man's best
   interests 103–5
  Hadith criticism and 96
  Hadith reports on hidden imam
   and 77
  infallibility of imams 59–60
  knowledge of imams 61–2
  man's acts 105–6
  miracles 67–8
  modern views concerning his
   contribution to 83

  nature of Qur'an 101
  necessity of imamate 58, 77–8
  non-appearance of Mahdi 76–81
  occultation of twelfth
   imam/Mahdi 55–6, 76, 78–9
  pre-existence of the soul 71–5
  rationalist approach to 15, 29,
   95, 135–6
  role of reason 95–6
  sinful believer status 108–9
  state of imams after death 68–70
  theory of the "four elements" 95
Muhammad b. 'Abdallah (The Pure
 Soul) 48–9, 50
Muhammad the Prophet 59
 authority of Hadith 3
 designation of 'Ali at Ghadir
  Khumm 38–9
 infallibility 59
 legacy to Imamism 7
Mu'izz al-Dawla 19, 20
Murtada, Sharif 21, 29, 77
mut'a (temporary marriage) 111, 131,
 132
Mutawakkil 133
Mu'tazilism 48
 'Ali's imamate and 36, 42, 44
 doctrine of justice and necessity of
  imamate question 58
 God's imposition of commands and
  prohibitions as justice 104
  doctrine relating to free choice
   105–6
 Hanbalis and 24–5
 Imami doctrine of return to life and
  110
 influence and rise of 22–3, 84
 miracles by imams and 67
 monotheism, emphasis on
  transcendence of God 85–6
 proof of Mahdi's identity and 81–2
 reason, role of 84–5
  reactions against 89

Nahj al-balagha ("The Path of
 Rhetoric") 21

naqib of Baghdad, 'Alid 20–1
naskh (abrogation)
    and *bada'* (change of divine decree)
        102
nass 2, 31, *see* designation
necessity of the imamate, doctrine of
    3, 12, 56–8, 77–8, 136
Nu'mani 51–2
Nusayri Shi'ism 72

occultation, doctrine of 2, 10–12,
    51–3
    continued invisibility of Mahdi and
        79–81
    in traditionalist Imami theology
        75–6
    impact on Imami traditionalism 15
    messianism and 5
    Mu'tazili attack upon 56
    necessity of imamate theory and
        77–8
    problem of new cases during 119,
        137
    proof of Mahdi's identity 81–2
    purpose of imam's existence in
        78–9
    taxes, collection and distribution of,
        and 129

Paradise 104, 108
"Perfection of Religion and the
        Completion of Grace in
        Confirming the Occultation
        and Removing Confusion,
        The" 52
pilgrimage 69–70, 133
political quietism of 'Alids and Imamis
    5–7
predestination and free will 106–7,
    see determination
prescribed penalties, execution of
    124–5
Prophet's descendants and *khums* 128,
    129
Prophetic practice (Sunna) 65, 112
punishment, divine

eternal, in Mu'tazili theology 87–8
    in this life, Imami Hadith 108
    in *barzakh* (purgatory), Mufid's view
        108–9
    "the promise and the threat"
        principle 87
    "in the grave", "torment of the
        grave" doctrine 91, 109
    "return to life" doctrine and 110
Purgatory and Hell 108

Qa'im *see* Mahdi
Qadir 24–5, 27
Qadiri creed 25
Qaramita of Bahrain 26
qiyas (reasoning by analogy) 115, 116,
    119, 120
quietist and legalist Shi'i trend,
    Imamism as 5–6
Qumm 94
Qummi scholar(s) 15, 28, 75
Qur'an 3, 112
    as created, or spoken, word of God
        86, 91, 99
        Imami theology and 100–1
    completeness debate 63–7
    Hadith and contradictory
        statements 96, 114
    Imami doctrine of imamate and 7
    revelation and interpretation 15,
        85
        'Ali's designation and 39–42
    statements on
        jinn 68
        marriage 131
        miracles 82
        obedience to leaders 57–8
        taxes as ritual duties 127
Qur'anic verses
    (03: 37) 82
    (04: 24) 131
    (04: 59) 57–8
    (05: 3) 40
    (05: 67) 40, 41
    (28: 7) 82
    (72: 1–2) 68

Radi, Sharif 21

raj'a (return to life) 109–10, 136

reason, its role

in the defense of traditional Imami doctrine 29, 52, 76, 95–6

in early Imamism 91–4

in Imami Hadith criticism 96–8, 117

opposition to use of 15, 24, 89, 94

revelation and 29, 58, 83, 84–5, 91–4, 95–6

as a source in Imami jurisprudence 119–20, 137

reasoning by analogy 115, 119

"Refinement of Legal Decisions, The" 111

religious authority

Imami scholars/jurists 116, 121

Sunni scholars 112

Sunni and Shi'i views compared 2–4, 34, 112–13

revelation and reason 29, 58, 83, 84–5, 91–4, 95–6

al-Rida, 'Ali 47

ritual practices

as emblems of Imami identity 130–2

pilgrimage 69–70

payment of taxes 127

visiting shrines of the imams 132–4

washing of feet 111–12

Rummani 28

al-Sadiq, Ja'far 2, 5, 48, 49, 80

Safavid dynasty 6

safir, sifara (representative, representation) of hidden imam 11, 17

salvation

as reward to believers 104

faith, good works and 107

Imami belief in twelve imams and 31

Imami legalism, gnosticism and 8–9

imams' intercessory role 107–8, 136

Samaritanism 5

"seal of prophets, the" 60–1

Shalmaghani 72

shari'a (revealed law) 2

execution of penalties prescribed by 124

theory of salvation and 8, 31, 104, 107–8

Shi'ism *see* Imami Shi'ism; Zaydi Shi'ism; Isma'ili Shi'ism

shrines 69–70, 132–3

Siffin, Battle of 43–4

sinful believers 108

sinners

faith and salvation and 107–8

punishment of 87–8, 91

sira (life story) of the Prophet 33, 35, 36

soul, the, debate on pre-existence of 72–5

"Sufficient [Work] in the Science of Religion, The" 14–15, 28, 113–14

Sufis 67–8

Sunnism

acceptance of juridical divergence 24, 56, 131

four roots of jurisprudence 115

function of miracles 82

Hanbali 24–5

historical tradition, 'Ali and 'Alids in 33–4

Imami Shi'ism and, divisions over authority of Hadith 112–13, 114

designation of 'Ali 38–42

laws of inheritance and marriage 130–2

Qur'anic statements on taxes 127

role of consensus 118

succession to, and status of companions of, the Prophet 1–4, 36–8

validity of *ijtihad* 44, 112–13
validity of juristic activity 15
theology 89–91, 105
under Buyids at Baghdad 21, 23–5

taqiyya (precautionary dissimulation)
7, 117, 124
taxes 127–30
temporary marriage 111 *see mut'a*
theology (*kalam*)
Ash'arism, Sunni 89–91
definition of *kalam* 84
early Imamism 91–4
Ibn Babuya's attacks on *kalam* 94
Mufid and use of reason in 15, 29,
95–6, 135–6
Mu'tazilism 84–9
traditionalism and rationalism in
Imami 14–15
"torment of the grave" doctrine 91,
109
Tusi 29, 111, 127
use of reason and revealed texts
137
views on *jihad* 126
twelfth imam *see* Mahdi
twelve imams 31–2, 49
Twelver Shi'ism *see* Imami Shi'ism

'Umar 36, 132

Umayyad period, Shi'ism in 4–5
unacceptable exaggeration 70–5
unbelievers, Mufid's view of *jihad* on
125–6
unity, Mu'tazili doctrine of 85–6,
91
Imami theology and 100
usul al-fiqh (principles of jurisprudence) 115 *see* jurisprudence
'Uthman 36, 43–4, 61, 64
later debate on completeness of
Qu'ran and 64, 66

washing of feet ritual 111–12
"wide attestation/multiple witnesses"
principle 68, 96, 116
works and faith 91
World of Shadows 72–3

zakat 127–8
Zayd b. 'Ali 48
Zaydi Shi'ism 1, 2, 23, 34
authority of imam 3–4
designation of 'Ali, position held by
39
Mufid's polemical challenge to
47–51
see also Buyids
ziyara (visiting the shrines of the
imams) 132–4

IF YOU WISH TO BE PLACED ON OUR MAILING LIST, PLEASE RETURN THIS CARD

NAME: _____

ADDRESS: _____

ZIP/POSTAL CODE: _____ COUNTRY (IF OUTSIDE UK): _____

EMAIL: _____

O N E W O R L D
O X F O R D

To ensure we send you the correct information, please could you answer the following questions:

In which book/catalogue did you find this card? _____

If in a book, where did you purchase it? _____

Which of these best describes your interest in our books? Please tick as appropriate:

- You use them for personal use or as gifts ☐   You are an academic ☐
- You work in book retail ☐   If so, do you have responsibility for selecting
- You are a student and our book(s) are recommended ☐   books for course adoption?   Yes/No
- Other reason? _____   If yes, for what course? _____

PLEASE INDICATE ANY AREAS OF PARTICULAR INTEREST

☐ Comparative Religion   ☐ Middle East
World Religions: ☐ Politics
☐ Hinduism   ☐ Buddhism   ☐ Bahá'í Faith   ☐ History
☐ Judaism   ☐ Christianity   ☐ Other (specify)   ☐ Philosophy
☐ Islam   ☐ Sufism   ☐ Popular Science
☐ Mysticism   ☐ Inspirational   ☐ Psychology and/or Self-help
☐ Other (please specify)

For further information, please e-mail us at info@oneworld-publications.com or visit our website at